LUCKY LAD

Local and Family History Publications by the Author

Thurstonland Township, Parish Chest Records 1695-1861
Huddersfield & District Family History Society Journal, Vol. 14, No. 1, 2000

A Population Study of the Upper Dearne Valley from Census Returns 1801-1841
Huddersfield & District Family History Society Journal, Vol. 15, No.3, 2002

Employment Statistics and Occupations in the Upper Dearne Valley from the 1841 Census Return
Huddersfield & District Family History Society Journal, Vol. 15, No.4, 2002

Distractions
Huddersfield & District Family History Society Journal, Vol.18, No.1, 2004

Stamp Duty Act 1793 – A Case Study
Huddersfield & District Family History Society Journal, Vol. 22, No.4, 2009

The Crigglestone Colliery Explosion – A Family's Triple Tragedy
Huddersfield & District Family History Society Journal, Vol 24, No.1, 2010

Living Conditions of Flockton Collier Families in Early Victorian Times
Huddersfield & District Family History Society Journal, Vol. 25, No. 2, 2012

LUCKY LAD

Memories of the
Upper Dearne Valley

EDWARD G. HELLEWELL

First published in 2007 by:
Graig Press
80 Cefn Graig
Cardiff
CF14 6JZ

ISBN: 978-0-9555978-0-0

Printed and bound in Great Britain by:
Proprint, Remus House, Coltsfoot Drive, Woodston,
Peterborough PE2 9BF

Reprinted 2008

Reprinted 2009

Reprinted 2010

Reprinted 2012

CONTENTS

PREFACE

After many years dabbling in family history I finally achieved the 'Gold Standard' of identifying all my 16 great great grandparents. Countless times during the research I rued not having quizzed the older members of my family, in particular granddad Hellewell and grandma Bedford, who were still alive when I was old enough to understand fully what they could have told me. It's not that I didn't have the opportunity to ask them pertinent questions, especially in the case of the latter, who lived on until I was 27 years old. From written records it's generally relatively straightforward, though possibly time-consuming, to construct a family tree, but this stark framework alone tells nothing of the life experiences of those ancestors. My one big regret in life is that I did not ask my two surviving grandparents about their own lives and moreover, what they knew of the lives of their ancestors. The volume of living history that I missed by not doing so simply doesn't bear thinking about.

I'm lucky to have 2 sons and a daughter who between them have produced 8 lovely granddaughters. It is for my own children and for the younger generation in particular that I've written down some aspects of my own early life up to the time I left home to go to university – almost the first twenty years of my life. I count myself extremely fortunate to have been born and brought up in a rough and tumble, but vibrant, textile and mining village in the West Riding of Yorkshire's Upper Dearne Valley. I was fortunate also to have been born a few years before the 2nd World War – a period of great excitement for a growing youngster. More importantly though for children of my generation was the 1944 Education Act. This single piece of legislation, although in many ways divisive, allowed me to be one of the first to benefit from a Grammar School education, which previously would have been denied – working class parents simply could not afford the fees.

The topics I've chosen to recall are representative of the wealth of opportunity, which my friends and I enjoyed in a less sophisticated, but challenging age. Obvious ones, such as my schooling at junior and senior level, are supplemented by accounts of a structured leisure time in orchestras, brass bands, the church choir, cricket, cycling and swimming as well as informal adventures and exploits with my mates. The years of the 2nd World War had a significant influence on my early life and I felt this aspect deserved a chapter devoted to this period. The final chapter describes my early working life straight from school and into coal mining, including my toil on the coalface. I've included some detail of the working method, because after a lapse of some 50 years the techniques of those days, so familiar to me, have now essentially disappeared. Indeed, it is easy to envisage that by the time my granddaughters read this book the once mighty UK coal industry will have vanished too.

Some lines of my family tree I've managed to push well back into the 17th century, my earliest traceable ancestor being born around 1600. However, I decided for the purposes of this book to limit the description of my direct ancestors as far back as my great great grandparents' generation. Although the depth of information I've found on each individual varies considerably, I've attempted to set their lives in the context of the times in which they lived. Details of those 30 ancestors will, I hope, bring my granddaughters closer to that one group of their forebears. If so, then the many long hours rummaging in libraries and dusty archives will have been worthwhile.

Memory can play tricks and in recalling events from almost 70 years ago it is always possible that I've made the odd mistake with a date, a place name or a person's name. Any errors, if they occur, are, of course, entirely my responsibility. The names of individuals mentioned in the text are not fictitious and if I have caused offence then I apologise unreservedly. To offend or cause embarrassment was never my intention.

It's quite possible that my young granddaughters will be somewhat uninterested in local and family history (as I was at their age) and will leave the book to one side. In later life, however, they might just wonder what the youthful days of one of their forebears was like in the mid 20th century. Hopefully, the memories I've recorded may, at least, give them some idea.

For my granddaughters Mari, Alice, Jane, Lily, Eve, Katherine, Amelia and Miranda with love

With love and sincere thanks to Angela for encouragement and advice and without whose help this book would have been so much more difficult to prepare

1
OUTLOOK MAINLY SMOKE

And it would have been so different for me if my maternal grandfather John Edward Bedford had returned to his prospecting and mining ventures in the goldfields of Coolgardie and Kalgoorlie, Australia for a third time as he had intended. Whatever the reason for his change of heart I can only conjecture. Perhaps his childhood sweetheart Ann, now in July of 1900 his newly wed bride, persuaded him that a small unremarkable village nestling in the Pennine foothills of the Yorkshire West Riding was preferable to some wild frontier town of Western Australia as a place to raise a family. In the event, my mother was born the following June in a small terrace house in Market Place, Scissett. My own parents Hilda and Timothy Hellewell never strayed far from this area and I was born a Yorkshire Tyke in a 'two up, two down' end of terrace property up Cuttlehurst Hill on the fringe of the village.

1936 was something of a momentous year – the year of the three kings, George V, Edward VIII and George VI - the fourth time in English history when we've had 3 monarchs in one calendar year, the others being 1066, 1483 and 1553. To add to the general confusion I was also born in 1936. My parents showed remarkable impartiality in the abdication crisis by christening me Edward George. If they really had wanted to be truly impartial I should have been named George Edward George. However, like all good stories it's simply not true. To put the record straight I was named Edward after my maternal grandfather and George after my paternal grandfather.

The village of Scissett hides itself away in the upper reaches of the Dearne Valley, which prior to the industrial revolution of the late 18th and early 19th centuries, must have been a pleasant and tranquil spot. In my youth its population was about 1500. Its modest elevation is such that arable farmland and deciduous woodlands drape both the steep southern valley flank and the more moderate northern slopes, which overhang the ribbon of industrial development and its associated housing straggling alongside the youthful River Dearne. The village is more than simply a product of industrial upheaval. It is the creation of one family, which dominated this small part of Yorkshire for over 150 years. Benjamin Norton, founder of the dynasty, together with his sons set up the first manufactory in Scissett around the turn of the 18th century. In common with many other West Riding clothiers of that time, through graft, craft and in some instances shady dealing, they transformed, almost overnight, a rural scene into pockets of industrial landscape bristling with tall chimneys. Standing a few yards from my parents front door I could look out over the valley and see no fewer than six fine specimens – some stone, some brick, some round, some square, some many-sided, some ornate, some plain. All had one thing in common. They filled the air with smoke of an immense variety of hues.

Although, by the time of my formative years in the mid-20th century, the influence of the Norton family had declined, it was still not possible to escape the shadow of the gigantic monuments marking their not inconsiderable achievements. Nortonthorpe Mill and Spring Grove Mill, each employing several hundred workers and built by the Norton's dominated the village. However, the fact that control of the latter enterprise had passed to the Beanland family and Cuttlehurst Mill, a further creation of the Norton's, had fallen into a ruinous state many years before was testament to the vagaries of the textile trade and the fallibility of even great mill owning families.

The three factors, geology, topography and climate, dictate more than any other influences the birth and development of industrialisation and in this respect the Upper Dearne Valley is no different from thousands of other industrial pockets throughout the world. Population in this area prior to the Industrial Revolution was confined mainly to the hill-top settlements lying to the north and south of the valley, the villages of Emley, High

2

View over Scissett from Cuttlehurst Hill, 1948. No smoke from 4 of the 6 chimneys, which could be seen from opposite my home – must be a holiday! I'm holding a model areoplane.

Hoyland, Denby and Skelmanthorpe, each one within a three mile radius of Scissett, being typical examples. For centuries the area had been active in the wool trade, as a cottage based industry typified by generations of handloom weavers.

With the advent of mechanised textile machinery it was only natural that the embryonic industrial developments were to occur in the valleys where fast flowing streams could be harnessed to generate the moderate power demands of the new small factories. It is therefore no coincidence that Nortonthorpe Mill was established on the site of a former water mill at High Bridge where an ancient river crossing existed. Development of the factory was then extended some 250 yards downstream along the valley floor until it finally occupied a site of some 4 acres. A second Norton enterprise, Cuttlehurst Mill, was established, also at the western end of Scissett on the flanks of Cuttlehurst Hill and alongside Bagden Dike, a tributary of the River Dearne. In addition to providing motive power, water was also essential for the various textile processes, dying, fulling etc and to achieve continuity of supply a series of three dams fed by a weir from the Dearne were built in Kitchenroyd Woods upstream of Nortonthorpe Mill. Three further dams were constructed by directly damming Bagden Dike to provide the water needs of Cuttlehurst Mill. It was as if the Nortons wanted a physical stranglehold on the village, coupled with a determination to prevent corporate invaders from infiltrating their kingdom along the valley from east and west, that they chose to build their third factory, Spring Grove Mill, at the opposite, that is, the eastern end of the village.

These industrial fortresses were, in the event, insufficient to prevent minor incursions and two lesser textile concerns sprang up in the village at Wood Street and Union Street in the midst of the Norton empire, whilst a further upstart established by Teddy Blackburn outflanked the defence and established a mill high on Cuttlehurst Hill overlooking both Nortonthorpe and Cuttlehurst Mills. Spring Grove Mill, strictly, is situated in the contiguous village of Clayton West, but its origin and close ties with Scissett

4

really made it part of the latter. As might be expected it was sited alongside the Dearne and usurped one of the dams belonging to the ancient defunct corn mill, Marshall Mill, lying close to the second River Dearne crossing, Scissett Bridge.

All of the factories and the vast majority of associated dwellings were built of sandstone from the outcropping Penistone Flags and quarried locally on the southern slope of the valley. Geology was crucial also to the further development of the textile industry in Scissett, for it was the numerous coal seams such as the Blocking and Whinmoor which provided fuel for steam generation so necessary to drive the expansion of the trade during the 19th century. Numerous coal pits were opened to exploit these reserves, but they were relatively small affairs, in the main situated on the south side of the valley, with the aptly named Toppit area providing several locations. The Norton's took advantage of their economic strength by opening the largest of these mines, which worked the Whinmoor seam essentially beneath Wheatley Hill from adits on Scissett Common, in Duke Wood and at Hay Royds. By the mid 20th century only one of these mines remained, that at Hay Royds, owned and operated by the Flack family. Nevertheless, tangible evidence of the former workings was manifest by the many spoil heaps and, in particular a large one, known locally as *The Pit Hill*, which still overhangs the village. Locally, larger mines had been sunk, each employing several hundred miners, the nearest ones to the village being Park Mill Colliery (my first workplace) a mile down the valley at Clayton West and Emley Moor Colliery up on the hills at Emley. Both were originally owned by the Stringer family, but became part of the National Coal Board upon nationalisation in 1947.

Coal also provided the raw material for the production of gas and Norton's were at the forefront of commercial exploitation. Gas works were built originally at both Cuttlehurst and Nortonthorpe Mills, the product in addition to lighting the factories was also supplied to the houses and other commercial enterprises and provided street lighting for the village. Gas production was eventually concentrated at a new works built at the eastern end of the Nortonthorpe Mill complex, this production facility remained operational well into the 1950's. Many Norton owned properties, my parents house included, were not connected to the electricity supply until shortly after the Second World War, and relied on the home produced gas. This is but one tangible illustration of the degree to which the lives of Scissett inhabitants were dominated by this one family.

Although the economic prosperity of the village stemmed from textiles and to a lesser extent from coal mining, two further significant industrial enterprises had also been established. At the foot of Cuttlehurst, a sizeable printing works had been established by Hirst Buckley and during my youth ownership still remained with this family. Occupying a site between Wakefield Road and the River Dearne, Firth Bros had built their mechanical engineering works, which originally served the needs of the local coal mining industry. The major industries therefore supported many shops and lesser commercial enterprises in what was a bustling and thriving village. Indeed, the large daily influx of workers into the mills from the surrounding area brought prosperity to the shops and almost certainly accounted for their number and variety.

The village centre was dominated by the large Co-op building, which housed grocery, drapery, butchery (my life long predilection for pork pies, sausage and black pudding I attribute to the early specimens purchased there) and shoe repair departments. Detached from the main building there was also a slaughter house – Monday morning playtimes in school were punctuated by the squealing of pigs being killed. Other sizeable grocers shops were owned by the Bentley and Morton families, the latter also operated a travelling van, which in addition to grocery, also dispensed paraffin. A second drapers and outfitters shop was run by Ernest Whittle. A favourite shop for all youngsters was Polly Wray's, which sold newspapers, confectionary and sweets. However, during the war sweets were in very short supply, which probably saved my teeth! Next door to Polly's shop was Isaac Wray's joiners and undertakers premises.

Somewhat remote from the village centre at High Bridge (perhaps the Norton's had some influence on its location near their mill) the Post Office and general store was run by Mr Jackson. Although the village did not have a doctor's surgery, Clifford Thompson's well-stocked chemist shop at the top of Wood Street together with the services of Nurse Taylor at High Bridge Lodge seemed to deal with all but the most serious ailments.

In view of the tiny number of cars, I now find it amazing that the village supported two motor repair garages – perhaps this is a reflection on the unreliability of cars in those days. Albert Robinson ran one garage sited opposite the church, whilst the Reliance garage was a couple of hundred metres away along the main road in the Wakefield direction. Both garages dispensed petrol from pumps with the filling hoses passing directly over the pavement to the parked car – this arrangement would now certainly be illegal. Willie Brook, who appeared to me as a boy to be the village's oldest inhabitant, ran a carters business mainly using horse and cart. He even retained a horse drawn hearse, although funerals by this time had become motorised. A vital business for the boys in the village was the blacksmith's shop situated at the bottom of Stanhope Street. Custom-made mild steel runners for home-made sledges could be obtained there, although frequently by the time these were ready the snow had already melted!

It seems as though the village had royalist leanings since those inhabitants fancying a drink could choose between The Crown and The Queen's Head and also in former days The British Queen. In addition there was a working men's club at the bottom of Sunnymead. There can be few northern villages without a fish and chip shop[1] and Scissett was blessed with two. These wooden structures stood in bleak isolation at the top of Stanhope Street and Fleet Street[2]. The former was run by Edgar Exley's family and the other by Jim Firth's family, both providing, in my view, high quality fare.

The pattern of streets and associated huddled housing, which I found in my youth was essentially that which had been laid out some hundred years earlier. Initial development had been mainly confined to the land lying between the A636 road, which had been opened in 1826 as the Wakefield and Denby Dale Turnpike road, and the River Dearne. This road is the main arterial road through the village. A series of parallel streets commencing with Wood Street, adjacent to the east end of Nortonthorpe Mill and ending at Water Street, had been set out perpendicular to this road. These streets ran down towards the river and it was within this area that the main housing existed. Several shorter cross streets of the same back to back type housing were also developed, examples being Dearne Street and Saville Street. The first industrial housing had been built by the Nortons in Fleet Street and Stanhope Street in 1830 and amongst the first occupants was my great great grandfather William Hellewell and his wife Elizabeth. These properties were demolished just before the Second World War following severe criticism for being a health risk. They were, nevertheless, something of a model for their time. Each house had its own well in the cellar, the overflow from one filling the adjacent along the row. The supply was obtained from a natural spring and eventually concern was expressed on health grounds because it was assumed that the flow may have passed through the graveyard of St Augustine's Church, being situated only a few yards away from the houses. After demolition, the site was roughly levelled resulting in a large rectangular patch of uneven ground strewn with stone debris and known to the local children as *The Ruins*. This truly was an eyesore, bang in the centre of the village. The displaced refugees from this clearance were re-housed in a newly laid out council estate of brick semi-detatched properties of uninspired plainness optimistically named Sunnymead.

The Nortons also built two long rows of houses either side of the A636 at Kitchenroyd, a small hamlet about half a mile from

The Wakefield to Denby Dale road (now A636) through Scissett, circa 1908.
Girl bottom right is my Mother at the top of Wood Street.

Nortonthorpe Mill in the Denby Dale direction. This small, tightly knit community had a reputation for being insular and viewing strangers with suspicion. The approach of any stranger or person of importance was always signalled along the row by one of the occupants hammering on the gas pipe.

Further ribbons of housing were developed over the years alongside the roads into the village at Spring Grove and along Wakefield Road as the A636 was known at its eastern end. Small housing developments also occurred at Busker Lane, Lower Common Road and at Cuttlehurst. The stone terraces which made up the majority of the village were not unpleasant to the eye, and by the time of my youth the light brown sandstone had been well and truly blackened by the smoke from the mills and the coal fires of the dwellings themselves. As a youngster, I never ceased to wonder at the subtle architectural differences between the various terrace rows, variations even extending to the outside earth closets, which passed for sanitation in those days. On calm days the valley was often shrouded in a smoky haze. Some 60 years later I can still taste the pungent mixture of soot, sulphur, oil and steam making up the atmosphere of those long gone days. Oft times the dense black smoke billowing from the tall chimneys would blot out the sun – a minor eclipse no less.

It seems to have been a particular trait of Yorkshire mill owners that they built their mansions in close proximity to the factories – almost as if they were afraid that, without continuous surveillance, an insurrection would occur spontaneously. Branches of the Norton family followed this trend by building Bagden Hall and Nortonthorpe Hall on the slopes overlooking the valley not more than 10 minutes walk from their enterprises. Both were built in early Victorian times, each being set in extensive landscaped grounds with the houses being approached past lodges guarding the entrance to long drives. These superb Victorian mansions said it all. They were above all else an expression of wealth, power and influence, not simply a place to live. Their occupants, supported by armies of servants, butlers, gardeners, grooms and coachmen, lived a life of absolute luxury, a stark contrast to their employees.

The soul of a place is not, however, in its buildings, its layout and its landscape, for these inanimate features merely form the backdrop in the life and death of people living there. It is the inhabitants and their actions, which form the community, although there is no denying that the physical environment has a significant influence on the quality of life and the character of the individuals in that area.

The population of the village, like that of the Upper Dearne Valley as a whole, was almost entirely working class, mainly employed locally in the mills or mines. However, a small minority did travel daily to Huddersfield, Barnsley or Wakefield for a particular job or trade, say in engineering or chemicals. Women formed a high proportion of the working population since there were many jobs in textiles, for example weaving, winding, and warping, which did not require tremendous physical strength and work such as burling, mending and sewing was ideally suited to female nimbleness. Life was indeed hard, with long hours, particularly in the mills, which typically commenced work at 7am and finished at 5pm. Many of the jobs both in the mills and mines were on piecework and neither slackers nor weaklings lasted long in this competitive environment. During the day the village was alive and exciting with smoke, steam and sounds of the mill filling the air. The whole village seemed to be bursting with energy. By contrast, at weekends the place seemed dead, dreary and drab. The Second World War and its aftermath were periods when the fear of unemployment had become something of a bad memory. There were plenty of job opportunities with every employer crying out for workers – a stark contrast to the dire situation existing between the two world wars when short time working was the norm. My parents and older people who had experienced dreadful hardship in those times often spoke of their anxiety, earnestly hoping those awful days would never return.

Historically, people of the Upper Dearne Valley are mainly a mix of Anglo Saxon and Danish stock each occupying their own villages. The exception is Cumberworth, which is of Celtic origin. Place names ending in *ley* and *ton* are of Anglo Saxon origin, whilst those ending in *by* and *thorpe*, Danish. The villages of Emley and Clayton West are undoubtedly examples of Anglo Saxon settlements and Denby and Skelmanthorpe villages of Viking origin. I have a theory. The intense rivalry between the villages, which in my young days often escalated into a punch-up between the young men, had its roots in these ethnic differences. In earlier centuries this physical approach to life and a roughness in attitude appear to have been even more marked.

John Wesley wrote in his journal on 9th May 1757 of his experience in Huddersfield, some 8 miles to the north west of the Upper Dearne Valley: *I rode over the mountains to Huddersfield. A wilder people I never saw in England. The men, women and children filled the street as we rode along and appeared ready to devour us. They were, however, tolerably quiet while I preached; only a few pieces of dirt were thrown.....*

The town of Barnsley, about 7 miles to the southeast appeared to have quietened down somewhat by the time Wesley visited it some 30 years later. In his journal dated 30th June 1786 he wrote: *I turned aside to Barnsley formerly famous for all manner of wickedness, they were then ready to tear any Methodist Preacher in pieces, now not a dog wagged his tongue. I preached near the Market Place to a very large congregation and I believe the word sank into many hearts. They seemed to drink in every word, surely God will have people in this place.*

In respect of the Upper Dearne Valley one local historian commented upon the brutal behaviour prevalent there. In the 1820's Skelmanthorpe was described as: A *village in which it was said that a whole man did not exist at that time, having lost fingers, ears and noses...*

Another local historian describing Skelmanthorpe Feast, also in the 19th century wrote: *Work was entirely suspended for a whole week and the savings of a whole year would be spent in folly and sin. The village green was a scene of wild confusion. The public houses were crowded with drunken revellers, who caroused all day and made night hideous with their quarrels and disturbances.* Sounds like a great place to me!

The most telling comment on the behaviour of my forebears must rest with John Wood of Denby Dale writing to the Revd Isaac Clayton on the occasion of the opening in 1816 of the Wesleyan Methodist Chapel in Skelmanthorpe. He wrote: *We have got a good and very handsome chapel. I hope it will be a blessing to the inhabitants of that place, for many of them want both civilising and humanising....*

Certainly, when I was growing up, things had, to a large extent, calmed down. Nevertheless, youngsters had to learn to fend for themselves and be prepared to mix it with fists if the occasion demanded.

So much in life depends on good fortune and chance. In my case I had two amazing pieces of luck. First of all, I could not have been born at a better time. That may seem an odd statement for someone who lived his early life during the years of the 2nd World War – a time of rationing and acute shortages. Yet those days were, for a youngster, a time of great excitement. None of my age group realised the great dangers through which we lived, but we sensed that these were historic, momentous years. Moreover, we could follow the action closely through the BBC wireless news bulletins, cinema newsreels and current affairs lessons in school, much as people today follow football. Timing for me could not have been better, for I was one of the first to benefit from the 1944 Education Act. This truly opened up the possibility of improved secondary education, mainly through access to Grammar Schools, which until the Act, had been largely denied to working class children of earlier generations because of cost. This one piece of legislation changed, at a stroke, the social and economic future of so many lives and, specifically for me, provided the opportunity to exchange an outlook, which was mainly smoke, to something potentially better.

My second piece of good fortune was simply to have been born in the Upper Dearne Valley. I honestly count myself lucky to have been brought up in what was truly a working class environment. Rough and ready? Yes, that sums it up nicely. But it was also a place full of optimism, full of character and full of characters. It was a place, which demanded hard work and graft, yet would reward such attributes. It was a place where youngsters were challenged and yet could enjoy life. It was the sort of district, which today media people would call vibrant. For teenagers there were innumerable opportunities to participate in the sporting, cultural and social life of the community with organisations such as football, cricket and swimming clubs, choirs, brass bands, church and chapel groups, and to visit the cinema and dance hall. These are exactly the opportunities offered by towns and cities. Yet, unlike inner cities, it had the advantage of being surrounded by fields and woods. Places to roam, places to play, places to dream. An industrial and rural mix - what a super playground for youngsters! That was my homelands.

2

AMONGST THE ANCESTORS

Revolution, Turmoil and Defection

To be who I am I need my past. A Northerner? Surely. A Yorkshire Tyke? Most certainly. A true son of the Upper Dearne Valley? Most emphatically. With 15 of my 16 great great grandparents living in the valley at the time of the 1841 Census I could never deny that heritage – nor would I ever wish to do so. Incidentally, the 1841 Census was the first to record the names of all individuals, their occupations and the places where they lived. In other words, it was the first time in our long history when we can be reasonably sure where all our living ancestors were and what they were up to. The list of surnames of those 16 ancestors has a northern ring about it, although it would be difficult to place it in the Upper Dearne Valley simply because two names on the list, Thornley and Mort, are typical of Cheshire and Lancashire respectively. Indeed, that is where these two ancestors were born. A further 3 ancestors in this generation were also born outside the district, but each one in Yorkshire's West Riding and none had to travel more than 10 miles to reach there.

It never ceases to amaze me how life is controlled by nothing more than random events. My amazement grows when I realise that a random event over two centuries ago has had such a profound effect on something, which today is regarded as almost God given and sacrosanct - my surname. If Lydia's lover had done right by her, then my surname would not have been Hellewell, but most likely Ellis. The simple truth recorded in the baptism register of All Hallows' Church, Kirkburton for 1799 is unequivocal:

W^m S^n of Lydia Healawell of Thunderbridge born February 3^d
Bapt 19th May.

With this dry, unemotional statement was my great great grandfather William's arrival in the Township of Thurstonland, some 8 miles west of Scissett, announced to the world for posterity. Who was William's father? I can't be absolutely certain, because the vicar inconveniently omitted it, in complete contrast to other illegitimates born in the parish at this time. Why conceal the identity of the father of this particular child? The answer, I believe, lies in the testimony, which Lydia gave before the Justices of the Peace in 1805. In that year she was hauled up before the local judiciary because she was either attempting to gain settlement in the Township or alternatively, the Overseers of the Poor were attempting to remove her out of the Township. Either way, her sworn statement is essentially her life history to that date. She had been brought to Thurstonland as a 6 day old nurse child by her mother Mary Dyson from the Township of Mirfield. *A short time after her lying in,* as Lydia's testament states, Mary married Paul Hellawell, who I presume to be Lydia's father. In 1798 when Lydia was 20 she was employed as a live-in servant to one of the local gentry Mr. Edward Ellis. She left his employ and went back to live with her parents a short while before giving birth to William. I know it is only circumstantial evidence, but I suspect that Edward Ellis was the father and his name was deliberately kept out of the parish registers on account of his social standing and the fact that he had been a churchwarden. It simply wouldn't do to acknowledge that an upright and respected gentleman was having his way with one of the hoi-polloi.

William was probably in his late teens when he moved into the Upper Dearne Valley, presumably to work for the Norton family, and it was there he met his future wife Elizabeth Mitchell. She was the first of my ancestors to have been christened outside the established church at Shelley Independent Chapel, just north of the Dearne Valley, in 1796. The Mitchell family had been long established at Bagden in Denby Township. I was at first puzzled why William and Elizabeth were married (in 1820) at the church of St. John the Baptist, Penistone, a good 8 mile walk from Bagden. Why didn't they marry in Denby Church, which was much nearer home? The explanation I found out later is a simple one. Denby Church was a Chapel of Ease and not licensed for marriages until 1854.

By 1830 William and Elizabeth were living in Fleet Street, Scissett and the Norton firm's record of the time listed William as a warehouseman in their employ. This occupation was always regarded as a desirable position and certainly above the lot of the weavers, warpers, dyers, finishers and other toilers on the mill floor. The family appeared to have prospered[1], for in 1843 William purchased a 420 square yard plot of land in Far Close, Kitchenroyd from a Joseph Senior of Denby Dale for 19 guineas. Whether William subsequently ran into financial difficulties or whether he simply received an offer too good to refuse I do not know, but in 1865 he sold the land and a dwelling house to Thomas Norton of Bagden Hall for £185. Elizabeth was somewhat unusual for her times, for in the 1851 Census she was listed as a shopkeeper – the vast majority of married women were non-earners staying at home looking after the family.

Also on my father's side, William Devonport Thornley was born in 1799 in Stockport, Cheshire and his wife Martha Mort was almost certainly a Lancastrian, most likely born in the Bolton area around 1802. There were, surprisingly, several girls with this slightly unusual name christened in East Lancashire at this time. From the family historian's point of view she was an inconsiderate lady for she failed to state her place of birth in the 1851 Census (the first Census to record that fact). Furthermore, she compounded the problem by inconveniently dying some 6 years before the next Census of 1861.

The couple first appeared in Yorkshire living at Kexborough, near Barnsley in 1826. They almost certainly travelled over the Pennines via the Woodhead Pass, a natural route between Cheshire and South Yorkshire, but the reason for their migration, other than employment, I am unable to conjecture. The baptism register of All Saints', Darton records the christening of their eldest son George and gives William's occupation as a weaver – presumably a handloom weaver.

Over the next few years they moved around frequently. In 1828 they were in the Upper Dearne Valley, for their next son, John, was baptised at Clayton West Particular Baptist Chapel in that year. In 1838 my great grandmother Ann Thornley was christened at St. Michael's, Emley, the baptism register recording that the family was living in Skelmanthorpe. By the time of the 1841 Census they had moved to Kitchenroyd and William was employed as a designer – a prestigious and influential job in the fancy trade[2]. Since they were renting one of Norton's houses at Kitchenroyd, he must have been in their employ. In later Censuses he gave his occupation as a warehouseman, something of a downgrade. Perhaps his vision and skills as a designer were inadequate to deal with the much more complicated Jacquard[3] loom. This French invention, in which the weaving patterns were controlled automatically by punched cards, was capable of weaving over 300 ends into intricate and subtle designs compared with the witch loom of 100 ends or the primitive treadle handloom of 12 ends. Is this an early example of technology creating redundancy?

Turning to my mother's side, Henry Bedford was born in the Township of Lower Whitley some 8 miles north of Scissett. He was christened in 1813 at St. Michael's, Thornhill, on the outskirts of Dewsbury, where his father Francis, according to the baptism register, was organist. By 1841 Henry had moved to Clayton West as schoolmaster and in that year he married a schoolmistress, Ann Hargrave, at All Hallows', High Hoyland. The marriage certificate gives further information about Francis's father, who is now recorded as a publican. Incidentally, an amazing chance find in the Calendar of Wills and Admons for 1920 (yes, a delay of some 40 years!) recording the grant to Isabella Bridget Bedford[4] the Administration of the estates of George Henry Bedford[4] and Caroline Bedford[4] who had both died at the Woolpack Inn, Lower Whitley in 1880 and 1879 respectively shows that the public house (still today bearing the same name) continued to be occupied by the Bedford family for many years.

By the time of the 1851 Census, Henry and Ann had taken up residence at the National School at Winter Hill, High Hoyland and were wealthy enough to employ servants. The school was built opposite the end of Hollin House Lane, mid-way between High Hoyland and Clayton West, and was deliberately sited there to serve both communities. The building is still extant and was converted many years ago into a fine dwelling house. Some years ago, I had the tremendous thrill of discovering a large sample of Henry's beautiful copper plate handwriting – he was the enumerator for one of the Clayton West Registration Districts in the 1841 Census and again in 1851. Henry died in 1865, at the age of only 53, from Phthisis, we know today as TB, a devastating illness, rife in those times. Ann Hargrave was born in Cumberworth Township in the Upper Dearne Valley and baptised at St. Nicholas', Cumberworth in 1817. Her father Benjamin variously described himself as a clothier and farmer. After Henry's early death she continued as a schoolmistress and two daughters, Louisa Ann and Margaret Ann, both followed their parents into the profession.

Also on my mother's side William Senior was the fifth member of this generation from outside the district. He was born in 1830 and he is the only one of this generation not living in the Upper Dearne Valley at the time of the 1841 Census. I first catch sight of him in that Census, aged 11, living with his parents Charles, a porter, and Eunice (spelled phonetically in the Census as Eunis) in Swallow Street, Huddersfield. His whereabouts then becomes something of a mystery for he is nowhere to be found in the entire Huddersfield (now Kirklees) area at the time of the 1851 Census. He surfaced again in the Upper Dearne Valley in 1854 when he married Ann Hinchliffe at All Hallows', High Hoyland. On the marriage certificate he described himself as a cloth dresser whilst Ann's occupation was given as a warper. Ann already had a daughter Clara born in 1850 when Ann was 19. Incidentally, Ann, born in 1831, was the youngest of this generation of my

19

*My great great
grandfather
William Senior
Circa 1875*

*My great great
grandmother
Ann Senior
formerly Hinchliffe
Circa 1875*

ancestors. In the 1851 Census, Ann and 3 month old Clara, were living at home in Scissett with Ann's father George and stepmother Elizabeth.

There is no clue to Clara's father but it is possible that William is the culprit in view of his disappearance from the Huddersfield area. Clara was certainly baptised as Clara Hinchliffe at St. Augustine's, Scissett on 12th October 1851 and her birth date was given as 12th December 1850 – unfortunately the father was not named. I can just imagine the vicar's disapproval and him writing, with some satisfaction, the words 'Single Woman' alongside Ann's name. However, in subsequent Censuses, Clara carries the Senior surname. Interestingly, some 20 years ago I saw a family Bible in the possession of a relative, the late George Senior. This contained a list of family members with their birth dates and Clara was included as Clara Senior. However, the fact that in later life she was known by the Senior surname in no way proves that William was her father.

I like to believe that William was indeed Clara's father and that Ann's parents initially opposed the marriage and forbade the couple even seeing each other. As a result William left the Huddersfield area, but periodically returned to meet Ann in secret trysts. Eventually Ann's parents realising that the couple were indeed deeply in love, became reconciled to the idea of marriage and gave their approval. It's a story, which appeals to my romantic nature, but wherever the truth lies, it is most unlikely that this small, but intriguing, mystery will ever be solved.

Turning now to my 4 remaining great great grandparents on my father's side, who were all born in the Upper Dearne Valley, the Mitchell name crops up once again. Noah Mitchell, who in 1841 was living at Bagden was almost certainly cousin of Elizabeth, mentioned earlier, and quite possibly her first cousin. At this time Noah was a warehouseman living with his wife Sarah Green, both having been born at Bagden. However, some 10 years earlier in 1831, the Denby Poor Law records show that Noah collected 2s 6d in dole money during that year. This period was one of the worst economically in the textile trade and no doubt Noah was one of many men who, through no fault of their own, found themselves temporarily unemployed.

By the turn of the 18th century, nonconformism was certainly making inroads into the Established Church and both Noah and Sarah were christened at Clayton West Independent Chapel in 1798 and 1803 respectively. I cannot determine how strong was their allegiance to the nonconformists, but the fact that they were married at St. John the Baptist, Penistone in 1822 affords no clue. In the early 19th century, marriage ceremonies were the exclusive preserve of the established church and Bagden fell within Penistone Ecclesiastical Parish.

An interesting sidelight on the 19th century treatment of the poor is provided by their household's entry in 1851 Census. A Thomas Mitchell aged 86, receiving parish relief at the rate of 2/6 per week, was living in the house, but his relationship to Noah is ambiguous. He was described as a lodger but he may well be Noah's father, although I have been unable to prove this.

My 8 great great grandparents on my father's side are completed by John Morris and his wife Martha Pell. Both John and Martha were natives of Cumberworth Township and in 1841 John was earning his living there as a fancy weaver. This was almost certain to have been as a handloom weaver working at home. Today, it is still possible to see many of the old three storey houses in Cumberworth and Skelmanthorpe – in days gone by the upper floor housed the handloom. John's parents, William and Mary, for some unknown reason, always christened their children on Christmas Day. John, although born, in either 1796 or 1797 was christened at St. Nicholas', Cumberworth on Christmas Day 1798 and his sisters Hannah and Amelia on that festival in 1803 and 1805 respectively. Martha was born in either 1790 or more likely 1791 and was also christened at St. Nicholas', Cumberworth on Boxing Day 1791, making her my oldest ancestor of this generation. John and Martha were married in 1817, again at Cumberworth Church. By 1851 the family had moved to Kitchenroyd and John was now working as a cotton warp dresser.

The surname Green has already appeared on my father's side of the family and it crops up again on my mother's side[5], although I am pretty certain that if the two branches are related the connection must be well before the 19th century. John Green was born in Skelmanthorpe and christened at Skelmanthorpe Wesleyan Chapel in 1824. His father Benjamin Green, a weaver born in 1804, never reached the age of 30 and his mother, Hannah Green (formerly Wainwright), remarried George Moorhouse. At the time of the 1841 Census, John, a fancy weaver, was living with his stepfather George, his mother Hannah, his brother Lot (13) and his half sisters Betty Moorhouse (8) and Eliza Moorhouse (1) at Pond End, Skelmanthorpe. John married Ann Shaw, also a weaver, at All Saints', Silkstone[6] in 1845. Ann had been christened at St. Michael's, Emley in 1818, daughter of Joseph Shaw, yet another weaver, and his wife Mary Townend. Money must have been desperately tight in the Green household at the time of the 1851 Census. Ann was out in the mill working as a bobbin winder leaving daughter Sarah, only 8 years old, at home acting as a nurse to her younger sisters Eliza (5), Mary (3) and Ellen (1).

The roll call of my great great grandparents on my mother's side is completed by Edward Liles (sometimes spelled Lyles) and his wife Hannah Dalton. Edward, born at Bagden in 1825, was christened at Clayton West Independent Chapel some 3 years later on 6th July 1828, along with his younger brother, Joseph, born in January of that year. The delay to Edward's baptism may be an indication that his parents were not regular chapel-goers. In 1841 Edward, a cloth finisher, was living at Bagden together with his brothers, John, Joseph and William with his grandfather John, a butcher, who at that time would have been 70 years old. It appears that Edward's parents John Liles, a farmer born in 1799, and his mother Mary Day, born about 1802, had both died whilst still in their thirties.

Edward's wife Hannah Dalton was born in Denby Township and christened in 1824 at Clayton West Particular Baptist Chapel. The Daltons seem to have been long standing nonconformists but changed allegiance from Shelley Independent Chapel where Hannah's father, Aaron, was christened in 1796. In 1841 Hannah, a burler, was living at home at Putting Mill (a small hamlet in the Upper Dearne Valley between Kitchenroyd and Denby Dale) with her father Aaron, who it seems was having a brief break from weaving as he is described as a shopkeeper, and her step mother Hannah. Her own mother Elizabeth Shaw, christened at St. John the Baptist, Penistone in 1786, died between 1828 and 1831. Edward and Hannah[7] were married in 1852 at All Hallows', High Hoyland. The marriage certificate shows that Aaron had returned to his long standing occupation as a weaver.

Family historians are always looking, indeed hoping, for the occasional scandal – a murder even, or some nefarious deed, but in that respect I've been disappointed. Throughout the whole of the 19th and indeed the 20th century too, it seems as though my forebears, like the vast majority of the population, stayed on the right side of the law. The same cannot be said of them in respect of the bed sheets. Ann Hinchliffes's illegitimate daughter Clara and Lydia Hellewell's seduction, together with several brides approaching the altar in advanced states of pregnancy show what a lively lot my ancestors were. Here again, they were probably no worse than the population generally and I have great sympathy with them, for birth control methods in those days were at best haphazard.

My great great grandparents' generation, more than any other before or since, lived through times of unprecedented change and upheaval – a period of revolution, turmoil and defection. It was the people of this generation, who experienced the full effect of a revolution - the industrial revolution that is, the roots of which germinated quietly enough mainly in the latter quarter of the 18th century. Nowhere was the change from a domestic system to a factory system more in evidence than in textile valleys such as the

Upper Dearne. Some of my great great grandparents were still working as cottage based handloom weavers - others had already bowed to the inevitable and been swallowed up in the mills taking up such jobs as power loom weavers, warpers, bobbin winders, burlers and cloth finishers. My ancestors at this time were overwhelmingly working class and all were employed in textiles, apart from Henry and Ann Bedford. As schoolteachers, this couple was the only one having any pretension to a professional status. The early decades of the 19th century were also a time of great unrest and strife. Early in the century, the Napoleonic Wars had cast a dark shadow over Britain and the aftermath was one of bad harvests, shortage and short time working. How my ancestors coped with these immense economic and consequent social problems I have no way of telling, but I cannot see how they could have avoided the widespread suffering and deprivation of that time.

These years were also a time of great political turmoil and the district was heavily committed to radical politics and to the Chartist Movement in particular. Whether any of my ancestors played an active role, I have been unable to discover. However, I do know for certain that even after the Great Reform Act of 1832, not one of my forebears of this generation had the vote.

The latter part of the 18th century and the early years of the 19th century was a time when the ancient religious order was seriously challenged and, indeed, changed forever. The established church had lost touch with the aspirations of the common folk and was seen by the newly industrialised workers as nothing more than defending the interests of the ruling classes and nouveau riche employers. The Upper Dearne Valley was therefore ripe for taking by the various branches of nonconformism and large-scale exodus from the Anglican Church was now a reality. The evidence from my great great grandparents points to a significant defection from the Anglican Church. Of the 11 great great grand parents who were born in the district, 5 were christened in nonconformist chapels, 5 in the established church and there was just one whose baptism I have been unable to discover. However, several of the families were somewhat tardy in baptising their offspring and often did so in 'job lots', which certainly leaves the impression that even the chapels had failed to stoke up much in the way of religious fervour and commitment amongst my ancestors.

Looking at the pathetic crosses made by my ancestors on marriage certificates in place of their signatures makes me feel very sad indeed. For me, it emphasises the most telling difference between my great great grandparents and myself. Their inability to read and write must have meant that the learning process was confined to an oral tradition, in which knowledge was passed from one generation to another. Such individuals would therefore not have the opportunity to undertake independent study using books and written material and their advancement in society was, therefore, effectively denied. In terms of my great great grandparents' educational achievement, as measured by the ability to write, only 3 could write their name, whilst 12 almost certainly could not. The latter all made their marks on the marriage certificates, although this is not an absolute test of their ability – the vicar may well have written out the marriage certificate in advance and simply assumed they were unable to sign their names. For the one remaining individual, I have been unable to trace any documentary record, which would indicate their writing skill. In educational terms, this generation of my ancestors might as well have been born in Anglo-Saxon England – truly in the Dark Ages.

The fact that they were born at the close of the 18th and the beginning if the 19th centuries did not make their lives any more secure than their Saxon and Viking ancestors. From the moment of birth they were in considerable danger from the manifold diseases prevalent at that time. They all must have had a fair bit of luck and been blessed with an iron constitution to survive the primitive ordeal of childhood – a hurdle which the majority of those under the age of 5 failed to clear.

AMONGST THE ANCESTORS
Hellewell Line

Great Great Grandparents

| William Hellewell
b. Thurstonland 1799
d. Kitchenroyd 1871 | Elizabeth Mitchell
b. Bagden 1795/6
d. Kitchenroyd 1864 | William Thornley
b. Stockport 1799
d. Kitchenroyd 1876 | Martha Mort
b. Bolton? 1802/3
d. Kitchenroyd 1856 | Noah Mitchell
b. Bagden 1798
d. Bagden 1867 | Sarah Green
b. Bagden 1803/4
d. Bagden 1876 | John Morris
b. Cumb. 1796
d. K.royd 1860 | Martha Pell
b. Cumb 1790/1
d. K.royd 1857 |

Married Penistone 1820   **Married ?**   **Married Penistone 1822**   **Married Cumberworth 181?**

Great Grandparents

| James Henry Hellewell
b. Scissett 1834
bap. New Conexion Chapel Barnsley 1834
d. Kitchenroyd 1887 bur. Scissett | Ann Thornley
b. Skelmanthorpe 1838
bap. Emley St. Michael 1838
d. Kitchenroyd 1890 bur. Scissett | Timothy Mitchell
b. Bagden 1831
bap. Denby, St. John 1831
d. ? 1906, bur. Denby St. John | Hannah Morris
b. Cumberworth 1833
bap. Cumb. St. Nicholas 1837
d. ? 1895, bur. Denby St. John |

Married Register Office, Huddersfield 1857   **Married Penistone St. John the Baptist 1852**

Grand Parents

| George Thornley Hellewell
b. Kitchenroyd 1864
bap. ?
d. Kitchenroyd 1949 bur. High Hoyland | Keziah Mitchell
b. Putting Mill, Cumberworth 1863
bap. ?
d. Kitchenroyd 1932 bur. High Hoyland |

Married Register Office, Huddersfield 1886

Dad

George Timothy Hellewell
b. Kitchenroyd 1901
bap. Scissett St. Augustines 1901
d. Cuttlehurst, Clayton West 1976
Married Hilda Bedford, Scissett 1932

27

AMONGST THE ANCESTORS
Bedford Line

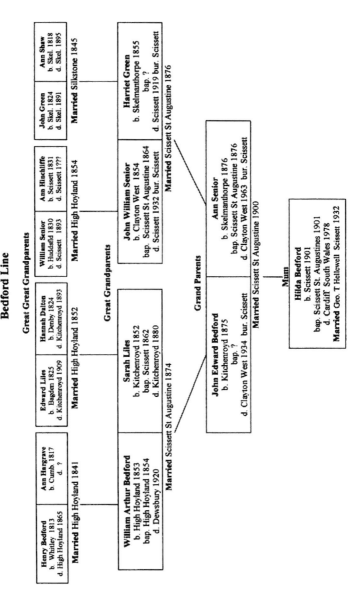

Great Great Grandparents

Henry Bedford	Ann Hargrave		Edward Liles	Hannah Dalton		William Senior	Ann Hinchliffe		John Green	Ann Shaw
b. Whitley 1813	b. Cumb 1817		b. Bagden 1825	b. Denby 1824		b. Huddsfld 1830	b. Scissett 1831		b. Skel. 1824	b. Skel. 1818
d. High Hoyland 1865	d. ?		d. Kitchenroyd 1909	d. Kitchenroyd 1893		d. Scissett 1893	d. Scissett 1???		d. Skel. 1891	d. Skel. 1895

Married High Hoyland 1841

Married High Hoyland 1852

Married High Hoyland 1854

Married Silkstone 1845

Great Grandparents

William Arthur Bedford		Sarah Liles		John William Senior		Harriet Green
b. High Hoyland 1853		b. Kitchenroyd 1852		b. Clayton West 1854		b. Skelmanthorpe 1855
bap. High Hoyland 1854		bap. Scissett 1862		bap. Scissett St Augustine 1864		bap. ?
d. Dewsbury 1920		d. Kitchenroyd 1880		d. Scissett 1932 bur. Scissett		d. Scissett 1919 bur. Scissett

Married Scissett St Augustine 1874

Married Scissett St Augustine 1876

Grand Parents

John Edward Bedford		Ann Senior
b. Kitchenroyd 1875		b. Skelmanthorpe 1876
bap. ?		bap. Scissett St Augustine 1876
d. Clayton West 1934 bur. Scissett		d. Clayton West 1963 bur. Scissett

Married Scissett St Augustine 1900

Mum

Hilda Bedford
b. Scissett 1901
bap. Scissett St. Augustines 1901
d. Cardiff South Wales 1978
Married Geo. T Hellewell Scissett 1932

28

3
AMONGST THE ANCESTORS

A Confident Generation

The next generation of my ancestors, my great grandparents, were well and truly ensconced in the Upper Dearne Valley. Indeed it could be argued they lacked ambition and were content to remain there - in biblical terms they remained in Eygpt and were *hewers of wood and drawers of water.* All were born there between 1831 and 1855 and all died there between 1880 and 1932.

James Henry Hellewell was my ancestor of this generation carrying the Hellewell name. He was born at Scissett in 1834, but his baptism at the Wilson's Piece Methodist New Connexion Chapel in Barnsley is something of a puzzle. If his parents, William and Elizabeth, had simply become disillusioned with the Anglican Church, as had many in the district, then there were surely enough local nonconformist chapels to choose from. Why walk from Scissett to Barnsley and back, a round trip of 18 miles on indifferent roads? It appears as though his parents really had been taken by the enthusiasm of the New Connexion gatherings, for his older sisters Mary Ann, Eliza and Elizabeth, born between 1824 and 1830 were all christened in that chapel on the same day in 1830.

James Henry was unusual in working class families of those times in having two Christian names. Sometimes in the Censuses he appears as James and sometimes as Henry. What did people call him, I wonder? A possible clue may lie in his marriage certificate. On such an important document, he didn't bother with both names but simply used Henry. In his younger days he was a blacksmith, this occupation being recorded in both the 1851 and 1861 Censuses. He married a local girl Ann Thornley, born at

Skelmanthorpe and christened at Emley in 1838. Whether the couple were truly fed up with the Established Church or whether they simply fancied a day out on the railway from Denby Dale to Huddersfield, opened just 7 years earlier, I'm not sure. Whatever the reason, they have the distinction of being my first ancestors to have had a Register Office wedding. This took place at Huddersfield Register Office in 1857.

By the time of the 1871 Census, James Henry had advanced to mechanic status. More than that, he must have been something of an entrepreneur, for he is also described as a *Coal Proprietor employing 2 men and 2 boys*. I do not know how long this enterprise worked or even the location of the mine, although I suspect the grassed over spoil heap in the field adjacent to Kitchenroyd Reading Room could well mark the spot. He too must have been a man of some originality and skill for, as foreman mechanic at Norton's mill, he took out 2 patents in 1884. Both were in relation to power looms. Patent No. 16271 was *Improvements in Looms for Weaving Looped or Pile Fabrics* and Patent No. 16272 was *An Improved Application and Arrangement of Brake for Looms for Weaving.* James died at the relatively young age of 53 and was buried at Scissett on 6th March 1887 to be followed into the same grave exactly 3 years to the day later by his wife Ann, aged 52. Despite his undoubted mechanical talent, he didn't die a rich man, leaving just £45-10s-6d, a modest sum for those days.

My other great grandfather on my fathers's side was Timothy Mitchell, born at Bagden, Denby Township in 1831. He was toiling in the mill for at least the first 40 years of his working life. In the 1841 Census he was an 11 year old bobbin winder and in later Censuses he's listed as a cropper or cloth finisher. Timothy lived most of his married life at Putting Mill near Denby Dale, but by 1891, along with his wife Hannah and their children he moved to be landlord of the Queen's Head public house in Scissett. Some years later the family moved to take over the Traveller's Rest public house situated alongside the main A636 road between Kitchenroyd and Denby Dale.

Timothy and Hannah's marriage flummoxed me for years. I had searched the civil registration index several times using all the variations of name spelling I could possibly think of, but turned up only one entry - a Timothy Mitchell, who was married in the Wortley registration district in the December Quarter of 1852. I already knew that his bride's name was Hannah Morris, for this name appeared on the birth certificate as the mother of Keziah Mitchell (my grandmother) born in 1863. Checking to find the corresponding entry for Hannah Morris in the civil registration index of marriages for the December Quarter of 1852 drew a complete blank. I was convinced therefore that the Timothy Mitchell entry I had found was not that of my great grandfather. For years I struggled with this problem, knowing only too well that many marriages never made it into the index. In the end, I became resigned to the fact that this was one of those unfortunate cases. In desperation I tried one final tack. I assembled all the information I had about Timothy and Hannah Morris and concluded that the most likely date of marriage was 1852. I now had the problem of deciding which churches were the most likely venues and, in order of priority, came up with High Hoyland, Cumberworth, Scissett and Penistone. For a fee, I then requested a search by the archivist of the West Riding Archive Service in Wakefield. Sure enough, the marriage of a Timothy Mitchell had taken place at Penistone on 25th October 1852.

From the supplementary information, including his father's name Noah, it most certainly was the one I was seeking. I was, however, dumbstruck to read the bride's name being recorded as Hannah Moorhouse. No wonder I couldn't find the Hannah Morris entry! I searched diligently the Dearne Valley Census returns for 1841 and 1851, giving Cumberworth Township particular scrutiny, for it was there in later Censuses that Hannah Mitchell claimed to have been born. No trace of a Hannah Moorhouse! Hannah Morris yes, the right age and in Cumberworth Township too. Their eldest son Noah was born just a year after the marriage and his birth certificate records that his mother Hannah Mitchell was the informant and that her former

31

name was Moris *(sic)*. Those two facts convinced me that there had been a mistake in recording Hannah Morris as Hannah Moorhouse in the Penistone Marriage Register. Who knows? The old vicar might have been an incomer and perhaps on the deaf side too - sufficient handicaps in themselves to be confused by the thick Yorkshire accent of those days. Of course, neither Timothy nor Hannah could read and so the error passed unnoticed and therefore uncorrected. Hannah was born in 1833 at Cumberworth, but not christened there until 1837, sharing the ceremony with a 16year old sister Mary and a 7 year old brother Jonathan.

There is still an unresolved mystery about Timothy and Hannah. The 1861 Census records their eldest child Clara as 9 years old, which would place her birth sometime prior to April 1852. The same Census gives Clara's birthplace as Cumberworth. At the time of the 1851 Census, Hannah is recorded as being *At Home* with her parents at Kitchenroyd, Cumberworth, presumably awaiting the birth. Timothy and Hannah didn't marry until October 1852 (some 6 months after Clara's latest possible birth date) and at this time Hannah gives her abode as Denby. She must therefore, have moved in to live with Timothy's family, most likely bringing baby Clara with her. This now begs the question whether Timothy was Clara's father. There is now no way of solving this mystery. Incidentally, Clara must have travelled through life without a birth certificate, since her birth was never registered.

In affectionate remembrance of Hannah the beloved wife of Timothy Mitchell is the beginning of a long inscription on rather a fine monument in Denby Churchyard. Further words are a stark testament to the fragility of life even as late as the end of the 19th century. By 1906, when Timothy died, he had already lost Hannah aged 62 in 1895, and within a few months of her death, daughter Jemimah (29), daughter Annie (18) and grandson Fred (17) whilst son Noah (34) had already died in 1888 and daughter Elizabeth (42) in 1899.

It is always said that one should invest or work in bread, beer or 'baccy' and the latter two seem to have worked for Timothy. His estate was worth £271-2s-1d, a tidy sum indeed, in Edwardian times.

I've never been sure what to make of William Arthur Bedford, one of my great grandfathers on my mother's side. Of all my known ancestors, he was the only one to have been born into anything remotely approaching a middle class home. By the time of his birth at High Hoyland School House in 1853, his parents, both teachers, were affluent enough to employ servants and he would certainly have had every chance to progress educationally and even enter a profession. Indeed, his elder brother Thomas became a consulting chemist and sisters Margaret Ann and Louisa Ann became teachers. Quite the contrary, he seems to have spurned the opportunity and as a 20 year old at the time of his marriage at St. Augustine's, Scissett in 1874, he was employed as a warehouseman in the mill. He was, however, able to sign the register, in contrast to his bride Sarah Liles, who made her mark. Sarah had just turned 21 years old and was carrying the only child of the union, my grandfather John Edward Bedford, born 3 months after the wedding.

Sadly, Sarah died of Phthisis in 1880 and in the Census a year later, 6 year old John Edward is recorded living with Sarah's parents at Kitchenroyd. William Arthur Bedford, for whatever reason I do not know, scuttled off out of the district and in the 1881 Census[1] he was a blanket raiser, lodging with a Thomas Scott in Providence Street, Soothill, near Dewsbury. Whether he simply could not bear to remain in the district without his beloved Sarah and therefore abandoned his son will now never be known. Of one fact I am sure - he never returned to live in the Upper Dearne Valley, dying at Dewsbury in 1920.

John William Senior, my other great grandfather on my mother's side was the eldest son of a family of 6 sons and 3 daughters. He was born in 1854 at Cuttlehurst, the same place that I was, but he was not christened until 1864, the event taking place at St.

Augustine's, Scissett. I suspect that his parents had limited means, for in the 1861 Census I find the family as lodgers with Thomas Newton at Cuttlehurst. By 1871 the family had moved into their own home in Scissett and John William, now 17 years old, was a joiner's apprentice – something of a departure from the textile trades usually undertaken by my ancestors. In 1876 he married Harriet Green at Scissett Church and signed the Marriage Register, a skill I would have expected, since his father William was one of the very few of the previous generation able to write. Harriett on the other hand could not write and had to make her mark. At the time of her marriage she was not in employment and lived with her parents John and Ann at Lodge Fold, Skelmanthorpe. The newly married couple moved in with Ann's parents and were still there at the time of the 1881 Census. By 1891 they had become independent and with their 3 daughters were living at Crown Street, Scissett.

John William worked throughout his life as a joiner and cabinet maker. Some of his pieces - cupboards, boxes and occasional tables for instance, are finely carved and display his considerable talent in that direction. I am proud that some of his works are still in my possession. John William was also a talented singer, appearing as tenor soloist in local oratorio performances. John William didn't have the musical stature of his brother, the remarkably named Festus. Family tradition has it that Festus performed as a principal tenor with the D'Oyly Carte Opera Company and also in the Berlin Opera. Whether the latter is true I cannot be sure, but it is certain that he did spend some time in Germany.

As something of a digression, I often wonder what prompted his parents to choose such an exotic name and one positively out of the ordinary in the Upper Dearne Valley. There was a Festus who was governor of Caesarea at the time the Apostle Paul was imprisoned there and in the third century AD a Latin grammarian of that name was living at what is now Narbonne, France. The most likely suspect and inspiration, however, is the little known

Saint Festus, who was imprisoned and martyred in the persecutions of Diocletian in the 4th century AD.

This generation of my ancestors mainly lived through the second half of the 19th century – a period when Great Britain and its empire was at the zenith of world domination. Britain, apart from its involvement in the Crimean War in the mid 1850's and a few skirmishes in its colonial territories, had been untroubled and unchallenged since the defeat of Napoleon. Britain was the world leader in new technologies and exported its products throughout the world. The Great Exhibition of 1851 was a proud showcase of achievement, allowing the country's enterprises, from the smallest to the largest, a place before an audience from across the world. Of local interest, Norton's were one of the exhibitors.

Although there were many developments in this period, these were evolutionary, in contrast to the revolutionary changes of the previous half century. For example, the railways, which in the mid 1820's and 30's had revolutionised the country's method of transport, did not develop on a significant scale until the passing of the Railway Clauses Consolidation Act of 1845. From that point in time the railway development was evolutionary, but it resulted in an extensive rail network, which allowed the masses cheap travel for the first time.

This generation saw gradual male enfranchisement, begun by the great Reform Act of 1832. Incredible isn't it, for someone writing at the beginning of the 21st century with all the freedoms now enjoyed, to imagine what it was like for women who had virtually no political influence. It was a wait of almost 100 years after the 1832 Act before their aspirations were fulfilled. A huge step forward in respect of the status of women, in the material sense, resulted from The Married Women's Property Act of 1882. Prior to the Act, women were essentially chattels. Anything that was considered theirs belonged strictly in law to their husbands. Following the 1882 Act, women were able to own property in their own right.

The second half of the 19th century was, above all, the Victorian period of political calm, a period of consolidation, which built on the achievements and foundations laid by the previous generation. My great grandparents must surely have believed that the ordered world, as they saw it, would never change. How wrong they were! Bismarck's unification of the German states in the 1860's saw to that. The humiliating defeat of the French in the Franco-Prussian war of 1870 was a portend of the terrible mechanised slaughter of the 1st World War as the 20th century was getting into its stride.

4
AMONGST THE ANCESTORS

Within Living Memory

My grandparents' generation is within my living memory, although my maternal grandfather and my paternal grandmother died before I was born. In many respects, to me this generation is almost as remote as my earlier ancestors. In reality my knowledge of them is sketchy. Yes, it's true that I knew two of them. After some 50 years I can still recall how they looked, how they dressed, how they spoke, but I still don't know much about their lives, particularly the time before I knew them. It's my fault of course, I should have enquired far more deeply into their lives – I know they would not have resented it. What's more, I should have taken the opportunity to delve into the earlier generations through their direct connection. I always remember my grandfather Hellewell telling me that, as a young boy, he chatted to old men, who had fought in the Napoleonic Wars. How much living history has passed me by doesn't bear thinking about, and I confess that the opportunity missed is my one big regret in life.

Every time I walk into my study I'm in the presence of my grandfather George Thornley Hellewell. On the wall is a framed head and shoulders portrait of him. He has an aristocratic face with definite Germanic looks – Bismarck almost, but with a thin slightly aquiline nose. I'm always drawn to his eyes – small but with penetrating gaze, from under bushy eyebrows. Alongside his portrait is an illuminated framed certificate, done specially for him. The inscription: *Presented To George Thornley Hellewell On the occasion of his 80th birthday by the Employees and Staff of G.H. Norton & Co. Ltd to commemorate his long and continuing association with the Firm and as a token of respect and esteem* misses one vital fact – the actual length of service he had given. To remedy this, I can remember as a boy the small silver plaque bearing the dates *OCTOBER 29TH 1873 TO OCTOBER 29TH 1944* being carefully tacked to the frame. The latter date marked a career of exactly 71 years in the Norton family's cause. That, in itself, was a remarkable achievement, but when he died on 10th October 1949 he was still in harness and he had stretched out his faithful service to a few days short of 76 years. Absolutely incredible! Do they build them like that now?

My grandfather George Thornley Hellewell
1928

When I was with him as a boy, I sensed that I was in the presence of an exceptional individual. He was a truly remarkable man, who had started in the mill as a young boy on his 9th birthday on 29th October 1873 and had risen entirely by his own efforts, through private study and undoubted tenacity, to become not only the mill manager but also the manager of Norton's extensive estates. He was indeed the prime minister of the Norton Empire. His father James Henry was the foreman mechanic in the mill, but he died a young 53 in 1887 leaving George Thornley, only 22 years old, to step into his shoes. This position, clearly, set him on the managerial path. I know that he was a hard taskmaster who expected the highest standards from his charges. Many men who worked for him have recounted to me his habit of standing at the mill gate in the early morning, pocket watch in hand. Those failing to meet the 7am start time were sent back home and in consequence missed a day's wages, a very severe punishment in those hard times. On the other hand, I was told he was fair in his dealings with the employees and would do his utmost to help people who were in genuine difficulty.

To his own family he showed no favours. I love the story of his unmarried daughter, my aunt Amy Keziah, a weaver in the mill in the 1930's, who on being sent home a second time was so incensed she refused to go to work ever again. She was a stubborn individual and one of the few to get the better of him. Of course, he had to pay for her keep at home, although she did her bit by organising the house, working alongside the servants in his employ. To my uncle Henry (Harry) and to my father he displayed not the slightest glimmer of nepotism. Both started as apprentice mechanics at Norton's and he expected them to make their own way in the world, just as he had done. He could easily have afforded to pay for them at grammar or boarding school, but he didn't even give them that advantage. They received just basic elementary education in the village school and started work immediately upon qualifying for a Labour Certificate at the age of 13.

My grandfather's leadership qualities seemed to come to the fore quite early in life. A 1938 newspaper report of his 65 years with the Norton firm mentions that in his younger days he was a keen sportsman, captaining, for a number of years, both Nortonthorpe Rugby Club and Nortonthorpe Soccer Club. Undoubtedly, he was a very capable and competent engineer with an inventive mind, for that same newspaper report tersely states *Mr Hellewell brought out many patents.*

Of my paternal grandmother, Keziah, I know simply the bare facts of her life and I posses but one small photograph of her. This shows a small white haired lady dressed in black, sitting in a folding canvas chair in the garden of the mill manager's house at Kitchenroyd, which was occupied by her and my grandfather for many years. Incidentally, my spinster aunt Amy Keziah continued to live there on her own, as a grace and favour arrangement, until her death in 1959. I never knew my grandmother Keziah since she died in 1932, some 4 years before I arrived on the scene. Keziah is a pretty rare name, even in Victorian England, but the fact that she had a sister Jemimah suggests an Old Testament inspiration, for these were the names of the prophet Job's daughters. She was born Keziah Mitchell at Putting Mill in 1863 daughter of Timothy and Hannah and during her early life she worked as a weaver at Norton's. At the time of her marriage to my grandfather, which took place at Huddersfield Register Office in 1886, she was living at the Queen's Head Inn in Scissett where her father Timothy was now the landlord.

I have always felt a very strong affinity with my maternal grandfather John Edward Bedford, who as a young man showed tremendous spirit and sense of adventure in setting off from Kitchenroyd, alone as far as I can make out, to prospect for gold in the newly discovered gold fields of Kalgoorlie and Coolgardie in Western Australia. A photograph of a young man in his twenties brings me close to him. He's alone in that photograph, somewhere in the vast Australian Continent. He's a slim, thin-faced figure with piercing eyes, wearing a waistcoat and wide-brimmed cowboy style hat and carrying a percussion rifle. Sadly, I never knew him for he died in 1934, some 2 years before I was born. He had an inauspicious start in life, his mother, Sarah, dying when he was 5 years old. His father William Arthur left the district, never to return, and he was brought up essentially as an orphan with his grandparents Edward and Hannah Liles at Kitchenroyd. I first realised that there was something odd about his background when I began work underground at Park Mill Colliery, Clayton West. Older miners, who had known him, on meeting me for the first time, invariably commented *oh, then*

My grandmother Keziah Hellewell (formerly Mitchell)
Circa 1930

you're Johnny Liles grandson. Indeed, he was better known in the district by the surname Liles rather than his proper surname, Bedford.

The little I know about John Edward is, in the main, what has been passed on by my grandmother, Ann. I truly regret not having rummaged through her memories much more than I did. What's more, I can claim no mitigating circumstances, for I was 27 years old and still living in the Upper Dearne Valley when she died. John Edward sailed for Australia in 1893 from Tilbury Docks and presumably landed at Albany on the South Coast of Australia before heading inland some 500 miles. He must have done sufficiently well in the gold fields to be able return for brief spells back in England in 1896 and 1899. It was on the latter visit that Ann Senior gave him the ultimatum that his future was either with her or alternatively without her in the gold mines of a wild frontier town in Western Australia. Was his choice a difficult one? I have no way of knowing, but he did exchange the gold mines of Coolgardie for the coal mines of the Upper Dearne Valley and by so doing was able to claim the pretty Ann Senior as his bride in July 1900. Of his time in Australia, I'm left with just a few mementos. A gold signet ring engraved with the word *Coolgardie*, a few gold nuggets, a fine geological specimen of quartz rock containing visible free gold and a 'porcupine' quill box decorated in typical Aborigine style are tangible reminders of those adventures.

On his return from Australia and after his marriage to Ann Senior, the 1901 census shows them living in Market Place, Scissett and his occupation is given as a 'Coal Hewer Below Ground'. Some years later he set up as an independent mining contractor with his own team of hand picked men. I believe that initially he did work at Nortonthorpe Colliery, owned, I believe, in the early nineteen hundreds by Hezekiah Tinker, an old friend of his. Little documentary evidence of his life as a mining contractor has survived. However, I possess a copy of a contract of 1915 to drive a stone drift between the Silkstone and Wheatlcy Lime seams for Messrs Stringcr & Son Ltd, which shows him in

*My grandfather John Edward Bedford when a prospector and
goldminer in Coolgardie, Australia, circa 1895*

partnership with Frank Stringer of Clayton West. A letter of 1927 from the manager, Mr Blyth of Park Mill and Emley Moor Collieries accepting his tendered price for a drift indicated that he was now working as a sole contractor.

He specialised in shaft sinking and tunnelling. Amongst his major works were the vertical shafts at Waterloo Main Colliery near Leeds, the original access drifts at Bullcliffe Wood Colliery near Wakefield and at Park Mill Colliery, Clayton West, a long stone driveage, *The Bedford Bord,* named after him. His final major project, completed just before he died in 1934, was an adit over a mile in length constructed to drain water from Emley Moor Colliery's workings. To this day, water can still be seen issuing from the adit's mouth in Benny Lane. Immediately after completing that contract, he had intended to retire at 59, a relatively young age in those days, but sadly he never enjoyed the fruits of his life long labours.

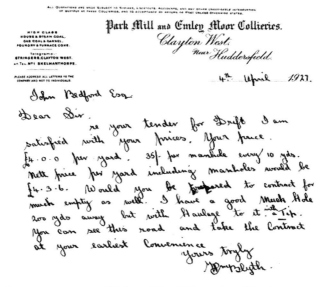

Letter to my grandfather John Edward Bedford, mining contractor, accepting his tender for driving a drift (tunnel) at Park Mill Colliery, 1927

He must have been an intelligent man, who was essentially self-taught. Apparently, for a man with little formal education, his knowledge of the geology of the Yorkshire Coalfield and his 'home' area, in particular, was exceptional. From him, I inherited a magnificent coloured section of the strata of the Yorkshire Coalfield and also many hand drawn geological maps he had made from his own field observations. Sunday evenings, my grandmother recalled, were his 'office time', when he would pore over mine plans laid out on the kitchen table and draw up a meticulous schedule of work for the week ahead. He didn't attend church or chapel, but on completion of his 'office routine' the Sunday evening was incomplete without him reading aloud from the large family Bible to who ever of the family happened to be present.

Joe Brooke, who was dayshift overman at Bullcliffe Wood Colliery, West Bretton when I worked there in 1959, told me many times of his considerable ability as a practical mining engineer. He was a careful, conscientious and knowledgeable individual, who always had the interests of his men at heart and in turn he was repaid by their dedication and unswerving loyalty. The mine owners for whom he contracted didn't have to worry about supervising my grandfather's works, for they had complete faith and trust in him and always knew that they could rely on him to complete a first rate job. Joe Brooke was uniquely placed to pass this judgement, for as a young man in 1927 he had trained with my grandfather during the time he was driving the access drifts to open up the Barnsley Seam at Bullcliffe Wood Colliery. This new mining enterprise was owned in pre-nationalisation days by the Bullcliffe Wood Colliery Co. Ltd. in which Joe's father and immediate family were the major shareholders.

According to my grandmother, he always tendered a fixed price for any contract. By adopting this strategy he was essentially backing his own judgement regarding the potential difficulties, which might be encountered, particularly in cross measure driveages. Poor judgement on his part could have serious financial consequences, whilst a 'correct call' could put him in the money. This explains the purpose of his detailed study of, and his own observations in practical geology. On every job he carried the full financial risk, for his men were happy to take a fixed wage each week with the hope of receiving a substantial bonus, which he decided, on completion of the contract.

He was clearly a prudent man, for he always liked to leave some earnings undrawn as an insurance against future unforeseen hazards. Every Sunday evening, apparently, he used to calculate his exact financial position taking into account the value of the work completed, his labour costs, his other outgoings and including materials already purchased but not yet consumed. I am fortunate that his income tax return for the tax year 1932/33 has survived, which gives an insight into his financial affairs at that time (the year before his death). His total earnings were £231 15s (£231.75), which today is equivalent to something over £43,600. His tax bill after, what appear to be quite generous allowances, amounted to only £6 9s 11d (£6.50), equivalent to a tax deduction of just 2.8%. My, how times have changed! One final comment about John Edward from my auntie May, who knew him well and was courting my uncle Colin Bedford in the early 30's – *"he was a lovely, gentle, kind man."* And that about a tough practical mining engineer!

My overwhelming memory of grandma Ann is of a white haired old lady dressed entirely in black, rocking herself gently in her rocking chair in front of a roaring coal fire in the single downstairs room of her stone cottage. I can't imagine that she harboured royalist tendencies, but where mourning was concerned, she certainly out did Queen Victoria, whose lifestyle after the loss of her beloved Albert, could best be described as hermit-like. The good Queen herself at least limited her seclusion to a few years and then resumed travel again around her realm. Not so grandma. After the death of John Edward, she resolutely stayed indoors or occasionally pottered into the garden of the cottage in Rock Villa, Cuttlehurst, which they had moved into shortly after they married. In fact, the only time I remember her venturing forth into a wider world was when I was a pageboy at

My grandmother Ann Bedford (formerly Senior)
circa 1905

the wedding of my uncle Colin to May Hutchinson in 1940. Her resolve to maintain this self-imposed seclusion was steadfast - she even politely declined the invitation to my wedding, despite having great affection for Dorothy, the girl I was to marry.

With this unusual approach to life, one could easily assume that she was a dull, self-centred, boring person. Not so! She had a lovely sense of humour and through the newspapers and radio she had a clear grasp of all that was going on in the world, despite her extreme reluctance to join it. From her twinkling eyes and her profusion of smiles, she was, I believe, a very happy person, who was content to live her life exactly as it pleased her. I know that at times she could be a very stubborn person. It's a tribute to my auntie May's sense of humour and even temperament that she was able to survive all her married life in the same house, particularly during the 5 years of the Second World War when my uncle Colin was away in the army.

Of grandma's early life I scarcely know a thing. For the record she was born Ann Senior in 1876 in a tiny house at Lodge Fold, Skelmanthorpe, the home of her maternal grandparents where John William Senior and Harriet Green, her parents, were lodging at the time. By the 1891 Census she was living at home with her parents and two sisters Ellen, 4 years older and Edith, 10 years younger in Crown Street, Scissett. She told me that she left elementary school at the age of 10 and then worked until her marriage as a worsted winder at Norton's mill. She once recounted to me the rare incident she had witnessed as a young woman from a window on the mill's upper storey. A large unruly mob had descended on the mill. Mr. Norton, the mill owner and Justice of the Peace, must have been aware of what was afoot and had the foresight to call out the local militia, The Staincross Volunteers. Apparently, an ugly confrontation ensued and Mr. Norton, unable to quell the mob, took the draconian step of reading the Riot Act from the office steps. A few shots were fired over the head of the crowd, which wisely withdrew without bloodshed. Although I cannot be sure, I think this must have occurred during the 1893 miner's strike, which was, in Yorkshire at least, a rather violent affair. Grandma lived through a period of ever rapidly changing technology on into the computer and telecom age, dying peacefully at the age of 87 in 1963.

My grandparents' generation left behind the unruffled period of Victorian assuredness to enter an era of unprecedented conflict and uncertainty. Never before had such huge areas of the globe been at war and now the technology was available to inflict severe human losses on all sides. The combatants of wars throughout the ages have always relied on the latest technology to gain an advantage and the First World War was no exception. This time it was somewhat different in that many technological developments driven by that war had a wider lasting effect on civilian population, including my grandparents in the Upper Dearne Valley. It could be argued that the advances in petrol engine design contributed most to the evolution of transport in the 20th century. Without engines of a high power to weight ratio, aircraft design could not have proceeded at the rate it did and as the First World War progressed the importance and the role of air warfare became apparent. This led directly, admittedly after the elapse of many years, to the massive civil aviation industry in the second half of the 20th century. Of more immediate effect was the development of the motor industry allowing the population to benefit, in mobility terms, through extensive bus services and to a lesser extent through ownership of the private motor car.

After the First World War, the Upper Dearne Valley was served for the first time by regular bus services run by Yorkshire Traction, based in Barnsley, and the County Motors, based in Huddersfield. The towns of Huddersfield, Barnsley and Wakefield could now be reached from Scissett in just over half an hour as well as villages along the respective routes. The private motorcar didn't have quite the impact of the buses, although my grandfather, George Thornley benefited in his work duties by having at his disposal the Norton Company car and was able to travel to the outlying farms of their empire and to attend business meetings held away from his mill office. Many times he would be picked up in the morning at home and driven the half mile or so to the mill.

Communications have always been of paramount importance in the prosecution of war and this branch of operations became critical when a war was being fought across the globe. The developments during the First World War in both wireless and telephony had a direct spin off in the period following cessation of hostilities.

The social fabric of the country also changed dramatically following the experiences of the war. Workingmen were no longer content to accept a class-ridden society, but many in the 'ruling' class did not readily accept change easily and were reluctant to concede the inevitable. Perhaps the greatest social change came about in 1918 when women over the age of 30 were given the vote. I find it incredible that less than 20 years before I was born women were almost totally disenfranchised. Even then, parity with men was not achieved until 1928 when the House of Commons passed, almost unanimously, the 2nd reading of the Equal Franchise bill, which granted parliamentary votes to women at the age of 21 – the same age as men.

5
HILDA AND TIM

Whatever adjectives could be fairly applied to my parents' marriage intent, 'impetuous' could never be one of them. After 'walking out' together for well over 10years they finally tied the knot at St. Augustine's, Scissett on 6th February 1932. Hilda and Tim (or Timmy), as the couple was invariably known, probably first met at Scissett No. 1 School. Their Labour Certificates, allowing them to enter the world of work at thirteen years old, states this was the Elementary School both of them attended. My Mum, being born in June 1901 started work in 1914, immediately after her 13th birthday, a little time ahead of Dad, who was born a few months later.

Like most girls from Scissett she worked at Norton's, first as a mender and in later years in the mat department sewing rugs. All her working life was spent there, only taking a few years off to look after me as boy. Yes, the hours were long; the work was hard, particularly on the hands and fingers, yet I know she enjoyed it. She likened it to being a member of a girls club, which met every working day. There, she could keep up with all the latest gossip and scandals. As the years passed by, many new girls started and the older ones, like Mum, just revelled at being in the company of youngsters and learning about the latest fashions and fads and, of course, the antics of the younger generation. Many of the group became very good friends, who stayed loyal to each other right through the retirement years too.

Dad also commenced his working life at Norton's as an apprentice in the mechanics' shop. I'm not sure who the foreman was in those days, but it could well have been my uncle James Henry, known universally as Harry, who was some 13 years older than Dad. Granddad, of course, at this stage had already been elevated to mill manager. The apprentice training which Dad

*My father
George Timothy
Hellewell
Circa 1930*

*My mother
Hilda Hellewell
formerly Bedford
Circa 1925*

received set him up as a very competent practical mechanical engineer. Not only did he become a skilled fitter and turner, but also he learned pretty well everything there was to know about textile mill engineering. This is a surprisingly broad field including the intricacies of complex textile machinery; looms, tenters and such like; as well as steam power plant and transmission engineering. Dad was one of the so called 'lucky generation', who were just young enough to avoid call up for the First World War, but also just too old for active service in the Second World War.

At the outbreak of the latter, because of his wide textile engineering skills, he was directed to work for William Whitely and Sons Ltd, textile machinery manufacturers, who had their works in Colne Road, Huddersfield. He remained with this firm for the duration of the war. For Mum and me, he might as well have been away on active service in the forces, for we hardly ever saw him throughout the war. For extended periods he was at textile centres in various parts of the country where he supervised the installation and erection of all manner of textile machinery, which had been manufactured at the Colne Road works. I still remember some of the places where he was 'billeted' for months on end – Rawtenstall and Waterfoot in Lancashire, Kidderminster in Worcestershire, Witney and Chipping Norton in the Cotswolds and Ashford in Kent. From these exotic locations, Mum would receive a weekly letter and she would pass on news of his doings to me. I always eagerly awaited his spasmodic homecomings, for he would always bring me a present, however small. I still retain, to this day, some instruments from a comprehensive boxed geometry set - much too advanced for me at the time, I might add. My greatest delight was when he brought home some wreckage from a German Heinkel bomber, which had been shot down near Ashford, including some German machine gun cartridge cases, presumably from that same crash site. These treasured relics were kept in the cellar at home for many years and I was mortified to find that Mum, without consultation, had thrown them out shortly after I left home.

At the cessation of hostilities, Dad was looking to move on and heard through the engineering grapevine of the vacant chief engineer's position with Brierley Brothers at Albert Mills in Lockwood, a suburb of Huddersfield. Hildred Charlesworth, the managing director of William Whitely, worked hard to persuade Dad to stay, offering him all manner of inducements – all to no avail. Dad had set his heart on being his own boss and running his own show in the engineering sense, and in doing so he would follow in the footsteps of his grandfather, father and elder brother. In 1946 he therefore took the position offered at Brierley Bros., which was one of the largest worsted weavers in England. His starting salary was £15 a week, a colossal sum at that time, probably 3 times the average wage. However, this came at a cost. He left home every morning to catch the 6.05am bus into Huddersfield and didn't return until the 7.00pm bus in the evening. Furthermore, weekend working, when particular maintenance jobs had to be fitted in, was a regular feature. In this new job I didn't see a lot of him – neither did Mum for that matter.

Several times he tried to persuade Mum to flit to the Lockwood district, a move, which would have cut down his workday enormously. She would have none of it. Even the temptation of a beautiful stone 4 bedroom detached house set in nice gardens (I can remember being part of the inspection party) failed to move her. Several times he toyed with the idea of buying a car and I well remember a series of offerings being brought for his inspection. In the immediate post-war years cars were like gold dust and the condition of many on the market, which had been laid-up during hostilities, struggled even to reach the derogatory trade term *'a good runner'*. The one I really fancied was a sporting vehicle, the Riley Gamecock. Sadly for me, Dad rejected the car option entirely and, although only 45years old at the time and despite there being far less traffic, I think the prospect of learning to drive seemed to him insurmountable.

By the late 1950's, the daily bus travel in all weathers and the long hours inevitably began to take their toll. However, what really finished his career at Brierley's was the strict enforcement of the new Clean Air Act. Inspectors used to tour the industrial areas (possibly they still do) with some sort of 'smoke densiometer' and using this device they'd peer skywards at the smoke clouds billowing from the factory chimneys. Smoke above a certain level of 'blackness' was only allowed to be discharged for a specified limited period each hour. These inspectors, who Dad likened to the Gestapo, apparently used to hang around outside the mill waiting to pounce on any minor breach of the regulations. He had many confrontations with the inspectors and he always argued that firing Lancashire boilers with Yorkshire bituminous steam coal made it well nigh impossible to fulfil the requirements of the Act. Knowing Dad, that was probably true, but no defence.

The management at Brierley's eventually made the decision to drive all the textile machinery, including the multitude of looms, with individual electric motors and therefore the magnificent Corliss valved triple expansion tandem steam engine built in the early 1900's by Pollit and Wigzell was put into retirement. Dad was, first and foremost, a steam man and he felt deeply unhappy with the new order. Salvation came when a vacancy occurred back in the mechanics' shop at Norton's. He was delighted to return to where he had begun his working life as an apprentice some 45 years earlier. Hubert Radley had taken over from uncle Harry as the foreman. Hubert and my Dad were firm friends and together with the other mechanics, including the mechanical genius, Bill Gunson, formed a happy team. Dad saw out the final years of his industrious and fruitful working life at Norton's in complete contentment – a nice ending indeed.

Despite his working week being pretty full, Dad was a keen sportsman and in his younger days, by all accounts, was a decent cricketer and rugby league player. After the war he still maintained his interest as a spectator in these sports and he had an encyclopaedic knowledge of Yorkshire cricket between the wars. However, his favourite Saturday afternoon outing was to the Fartown ground to shout for Huddersfield Rugby League Club, known throughout the rugby league world as Fartown or The Claret and Golds (the latter name now seems to have fallen by the wayside). He remembered and was inspired by the side known as *The Team of All the Talent*, arguably one of the finest club sides ever. He often told me about the legendary centre threequarter, Harold Wagstaffe, still known today as *The Prince of Centres,* and his left wing partner, the Australian, Albert Aaron Rosenfeld. In attack, this combination must have been the deadliest ever to take the rugby field. Rosenfeld's massive haul of 80 tries in one season is still standing after 90 years and now unlikely ever to be broken.

Both Mum and Dad were committed Anglicans and regularly attended at St. Augustine's, Scissett. Mum was a devoted Mother's Union member and Dad, when he retired, was a church council member and ended up editing and distributing the parish magazine, simply because no one else would take the job on. Dad put his heart and soul into this, just as he had done with anything he had tackled throughout his life. Dad always fancied writing and anonymous short pieces of his on topical ecclesiastical issues appeared from time to time – Dad was wise enough to leave serious theology to the experts. His secular literary desires were met by frequent contributions to the Letters Pages of the newspapers. The Huddersfield Examiner and the more exalted Yorkshire Post both received and published several contributions. However, the area's Huddersfield and District Chronicle, published in Clayton West and always known locally as The Advertiser, was his main platform. At the peak of his output he was knocking out at least one letter a month on an eclectic range of topics. He certainly had a brave heart, for he seemed to tackle almost anything and, as one can imagine, his letters occasionally attracted a fair amount of flak.

Mum was also a keen writer, but in her case she kept her opinions and news private to the intended recipients. She was one of the keenest letter writers I can imagine and she held regular dialogues with several parts of the Empire as well to places within the British Isles. Mum's enthusiastic hobby had a fortunate spin off

56

for me. As a boy I managed to build up quite a collection of foreign stamps. Some of the duplicates I managed to trade in the schoolyard, and New Zealand specimens, being noted for their colourful scenes, were popular swaps. I'm not quite sure how some of Mum's pen-friendships began, although in the case of her dear friend Mona Beatson in New Zealand it was certainly through the Anglican Church. St. Augustine's, Scissett is in the Diocese of Wakefield and through that connection she made contact with Mrs Beatson (she always referred to her in this rather formal manner) who then was a parishioner of St. John's, Wakefield, a few miles outside Nelson in New Zealand's South Island. It was a long, faithful and fruitful correspondence, indeed a true friendship, and finally I had the sad task of writing to New Zealand to pass on news of Mum's death. The other correspondents I remember were Jean in Brisbane, Australia, Lizzie in Kirkwall, Shetland Isles and Edna (Moore) in Millom, Cumberland.

It maybe surprising that as working class people born and brought up in the radical Upper Dearne Valley, both Mum and Dad were staunch Conservatives. The valley was natural Labour territory, but Scissett was certainly the exception, being split, I would guess, roughly equally between left and right. The village even had a Conservative Club, the only one for miles around, although, during my youth, support was waning and it became defunct sometime in the 1950's. I often puzzled why Scissett should be the political exception in this part of Yorkshire and, although I cannot be certain, the suspicion must be that the Norton family, as the main employer and Conservative through and through, exerted a considerable but subtle influence.

Both Mum and Dad had a great love of music, Mum in particular having considerable ability on the piano. Dad could amuse himself on the piano, but was hardly in Mum's class. As a boy Dad sang in St. Augustine's Church choir in the days when the redoubtable Tom Morley was in his hey day – when I joined the choir Tom hadn't long been retired from the post, which must say something about choirmasters' longevity. The story, which Dad often recounted concerned a choir practice in the vestry. Tom asked my Dad where middle C was – a question loaded with ambiguity. I assume Tom was referring to the musical stave, in which case the answer is the ledger line below the stave in the treble clef. Dad thinking of the piano keyboard answered "at the side of the keyhole" - hardly the answer Tom expected. Tom didn't realise the ambiguity in his question, nor did he see the funny side and rewarded Dad with an almighty clout. Dad, apparently, ended up in an untidy heap in the cassock cupboard.

In later years, Dad developed a decent tenor voice, but he never took this talent into a formal choir. His great delight on Sunday lunchtimes was to meet up with like-minded singing friends for a pint or two, the Travellers Rest at Kitchenroyd being a favoured haunt. Amongst the group were some excellent singers including Charlie Blackburn, Bertie Shaw amongst the tenors and the redoubtable soloist Archie Cook, whose remarkable voice was worth 4 in any bass section. The repertoire was eclectic, at one end of the spectrum were the sacred oratorio choruses of Handel, Mendelssohn along with Mozart's 12th Mass. Somewhere in the middle came the favourite hymn tunes such as Deep Harmony and Eventide. At the other end of the spectrum, choruses from Gilbert and Sullivan were laced with secular songs and carols. Irrespective of the rest of the programme, the two favourites, *Hail Smiling Morn* (a secular carol in a rollicking 6/8 time) and the Holmfirth Anthem, *Pratty Flowers,* were always included. I listened in on a couple of occasions and I must say the performance was certainly more than impromptu and the atmosphere could be best described as relaxed with serious intent.

For many years, Mum and Dad worked tirelessly for the Scissett Old Folks Treat. Dad was chairman of the committee for many years and besides fund raising throughout the year, the event took considerable organisational skills – arranging food supplies, then its preparation and serving, washing up as well as setting up transport for infirm ones. The main annual event was a 'proper' ham and beef tea followed by evening entertainment in the Parish Room. At the end of the evening the old folk received a present to mark the occasion. As Mum and Dad got older they both returned home exhausted, but I know the completion of another successful event gave them great satisfaction.

Memory is, of course, very selective and I'm only too aware that looking back to a time well over half a century ago is bound to be very subjective in terms of assessing the true character of Mum and Dad. Physically they were quite similar. Both had blond hair and both had rather finely featured thinnish faces – indeed they could well have been taken for brother and sister. More than that, their behaviour and general demeanour were alike in so many ways. Both were extremely hard working, God fearing individuals, who lived their lives according to the Low Church Anglican   tradition in which they had been raised. Not for them esoteric theological argument and discussion, but a life to be lived according to the ten Commandments. Each had a tremendous sense of responsibility to the community and never once can I recall either Mum or Dad having any dispute with friends or neighbours. Quite the contrary, confrontation was not in their make up and at times they would act as informal mediators if there had been a bit of a 'set to' amongst the locals.

For Mum and Dad, family loyalty above all else is the one trait I would pick out if pressed to summarize the one characteristic which would best describe them. Mum was devoted to grandma Bedford and not one day passed, holidays excepted, that she did not trot off down to Rock Villa to spend at least an hour in her Mum's company. I can only assume this devotion began with the death of granddad Bedford way back in 1932 and Mum felt it her duty to give comfort and support to grandma, who I think never really came to terms with her loss. Even after grandma's passing in 1963, Mum still continued daily visits to her old home. Uncle Colin, the baby of the family, some 13 years younger than Mum still lived in the house with his wife, May, and the three of them certainly shared a close bond.

Of a more formal nature were the weekly visits we made as a family to granddad Hellewell and aunt Amy Keziah at

A Hellewell Wedding 1940
Back row from left: my mother Hilda, my aunt Amy Keziah, my uncle Harry
(Bridegroom), Ethel Shaw (Bride)
Front row from left: my grandfather George Thornley,
my father George Timothy, myself

A Bedford Wedding 1940
Back row from left: my aunt Marion Hollingworth (formerly Bedford),
uncle Herbert Hollingworth, my mother Hilda, my father George Timothy
Front row from left: my grandmother Ann, Tommy Hutchinson, my uncle
Colin (Bridegroom), May Hutchinson (Bride)
In front: myself and cousin June Hollingworth

Kitchenroyd. Every Sunday afternoon, Mum and Dad would walk me through Bagden Wood to the mill manager's house. Usually uncle Harry and his second wife Ethel would also be there. I got on well with uncle Harry, but never took to Ethel, who always appeared to have a smell under her nose and never once can I recall her smiling at me. High tea would always be served and I was certainly privileged to eat with granddad in his study – why he always took his meals alone and not with the rest of the family has remained a mystery to me.

Temperament was the one personality trait where Mum and Dad were like chalk and cheese. Mum was, gentle, mild mannered and quietly spoken – to some she might even have appeared reserved, but she truly was warm hearted and loving to me. Mum, however could be quite a strict disciplinarian, but her punishments were always measured and fair. She knew exactly how to deal with a boy who occasionally got up to the odd trick or two and she had never to resort to the common threat "wait till your father gets home." Dad's temperament, on the other hand, could be best described as the short fuse variety. He could be roused to anger almost spontaneously and the ferocity of his verbal and physical attacks made me cower in terror on many occasions. Many were the times I needed Mum's protection and even grandma Bedford and auntie May had to intervene on several occasions.

One particular incident, which happened when I was 12 years old is still vivid in my memory. One evening, after playing cricket, I returned home a couple of hours later than I had promised and my attempts to justify this simply enraged Dad further. The net result for me was a purple cauliflower ear and a black eye. For the next few days all enquiries at school were answered by saying that I had been hit with a cricket ball. As the years have passed I've often wondered why Dad acted in this extreme manner since I'm sure that I was the only recipient and I'm absolutely certain he never even threatened Mum verbally let alone physically. I can only assume that my wanderings from the straight and narrow represented to him a defiance of his authority and this was his method of re-establishing his definition of law and order. Retribution was always swift, but mercifully short-lived. I certainly would not have wanted a sullen, brooding atmosphere lingering on for hours or possibly days afterwards. Although he never apologised to me, I know for certain (Mum often told me) that after such incidents he was truly repentant of his actions and normality returned to our relationship very quickly. I can honestly say that I have never held these incidents against Dad and as I passed into the teenage years our relationship matured into one of great respect for each other.

Despite the odd fracas with Dad from time to time, I was most fortunate in having loving parents, who simply wanted me to make the best of whatever talent I possessed. I enjoyed tremendous support from them in whatever activity I chose – boys tend to swap projects and enthusiasms with amazing frequency. Perhaps the greatest compliment I can pay them is to say that they had the good sense to allow me to develop in my own way from about the age of 14. No longer did they consider me a boy, but as a young adult capable of making my own judgements. Of course, they were there for me if I ever needed advice, but they avoided directly influencing me and certainly never imposed their will. I was by this time playing in a decent standard contesting brass band and much of my time was in the company of adults. Naturally, therefore, my attitudes were somewhat ahead of my chronological age. For example, in company with other band members I did let my hair down a bit after a contest victory, in my case with a spot of under age drinking. Yes, I enjoyed an extremely happy childhood followed by challenging and exciting teenage years – Mum and Dad saw to that. I'll be forever grateful. One can't choose ones parents, but in my case I couldn't have done better if I'd had that choice. Sheer good luck, eh?

6
HITLER AND ME

Of course, I never met Hitler, but I've often wondered if I had done so, would I have been so easily taken in by him as so many of the great and good were. History is full of *what ifs* and if our Prime Minister, Neville Chamberlain, had stood his ground there is no doubt that my life, and particularly, my early childhood would have been very different. As a two year old at the time, I don't remember Mr Chamberlain stepping out on the tarmac at Heston airfield waving a bit of paper, the Munich Agreement, which gave 'peace in our time'. The Agreement, signed on 29th September 1938, transferred the Sudetenland of Czechoslovakia to Germany. This land grab, Herr Hitler had assured Mr Chamberlain, would be Germany's final territorial demand, having already retaken the Rhineland from France in 1936 and annexed Austria in the Anschluss just 6 months earlier. In the event, 'peace with honour', as it was referred to at the time, lasted less than a year. Britain fulfilled its treaty obligations to Poland by declaring war on Germany on 3rd September 1939 in response to Germany's attack on Poland two days earlier. The war, which lasted almost 6 years, drew more and more nations into the conflict and covered the whole of the globe, truly meriting the title *The Second World War*.

I was too young to realise the import of these early shenanigans, but I somehow sensed that whatever was afoot would not be to my benefit. I remember an earnest discussion at granddad Hellewell's during one of the regular Sunday afternoon visits with Mum and Dad. The consensus seemed to be that Mr Churchill was the man for the job – looking back, I suspect that Britain had declared war that very same morning. Although I really had no idea what was happening, I realised from the tone of the conversation that these were serious times. Some months earlier,

I remember Dad and several neighbours digging out for an underground air raid shelter in the bank behind our row of houses, but again the significance was lost on me.

This modest under ground bunker, however, was to play a dominant role in my early years. My earliest recollection of the war - indeed my clearest recollection from childhood, was being wakened during the night, putting on some clothes and shoes and being walked out into the dark night with Mum and Dad into this supposed haven of safety. There, in the dim orange light of paraffin lamps, the neighbours were gathered together, sitting on roughly made wooden benches around the walls. The not unpleasant aroma from the lamps has stayed with me throughout my life. I was soon able to recognise the characteristic sound of German bombers with their rather rough, raucous, throbbing noise, which was quite different from our own planes with their smoother, even note. I experienced these sounds many times whilst being led out to the shelter. I always looked skywards, but never caught a fleeting glimpse of the raiders. The enemy bombers appeared to pass directly overhead on their way to wreak havoc on Sheffield, Manchester and Liverpool. Occasionally the district received a stray bomb or two, which had been jettisoned. Clearly, some attackers had encountered difficulty finding the target and were determined to scarper back to base with as light a load as possible. What terrified me most was not the bombing, but the tremendous sharp crack of our own anti-aircraft (ack-ack) batteries popping away at the raiders. We waited patiently in the shelter until the 'all clear' siren sounded and then back to bed for the remainder of the night. Incidentally, the siren emitted a wailing fluctuating note to warn of a raid, contrasting with the continuous tone of the 'all clear' signal.

The total blackout was the most immediate effect on my world at the start of hostilities. Every house had to ensure that not even the tinniest ray of light escaped during the hours of darkness. Woe betide any household which failed in that duty. Air raid wardens and home guard personnel patrolling the streets would severely admonish offending occupants and I believe that a fine could be imposed after several cautions had been issued. Mum hung heavy black curtains at the windows and a curtain of the same material was hung from a rail just behind the door out to the road. The latter effectively prevented light shining out when the door was opened. Similar curtains were hung just inside the doors of public buildings. I remember full well tumbling down the step through a blackout curtain and into Jim Firth's subterranean chip shop on the first evening he opened his new premises, having been taken there as a treat by Auntie May.

Walking out at night could be a hazardous and dangerous occupation, for all street lighting was prohibited for the duration of the war. Dense cloud cover truly brought home the meaning of 'pitch black' when nothing, not even a building or tree, could be seen in silhouette. Many people suffered injury as a result of colliding with street furniture, falling down road repair holes, tripping over uneven pavement flags or even just falling awkwardly, having missed the pavement edge. I looked forward to nights with a full moon and I still remember those occasions when everything was bathed in a beautiful silvery light and walking out was almost an ethereal experience. The stars shone like diamonds and since the war I've never seen so many stars; the insidious light pollution today is such that I'm unlikely ever to glimpse that glory again. Clear nights however, had a serious downside. Despite the Germans having developed radio aids for accurate bombing such as *Knickebein* and *X-Geraete*, nothing could beat the certainty of visual navigation to the target whilst executing the bombing run. Consequently, the frequency of raids increased in times of clear weather. In order to reduce injury from flying glass should a high explosive bomb detonate nearby, all windows in public buildings and houses were taped. I can remember licking the glue on the brown paper tape when helping Mum tape our windows. To me it wasn't too revolting, but then children can have strange tastes!

Food rationing was soon introduced and distribution was controlled by means of ration books containing coupons, which the shopkeepers removed for the items purchased. I honestly can't remember the quantities of food allocated, but I've been told since that these were indeed meagre. Men in arduous occupations such as mining and heavy engineering qualified for extra rations of meat and bacon. Lord Woolton was the man in charge of rationing and wrongly became something of a hate figure. Even then, I figured it a good idea that scarce food resources were, in theory at least, distributed fairly and no advantage given to the wealthy. Farmers, however, were in a prime position and although inspectors carried out spot checks on the number of animals, many undeclared specimens, particularly pigs, were successfully concealed. These illicit animals were secretly slaughtered and the joints of meat, hams and sides of bacon found their way onto the black market. Surprisingly, rationing continued in some commodities for some 8 years after the end of the war, the free market being finally restored in July 1953. It was during the post-war period that I remember Dad and uncle Colin collecting, under cover of darkness, from Stubbing Farm, hams and bacon sides - the latter being not all that lean and far too salty for my liking. Such clandestine operations were fairly commonplace and occasionally farmers and traffickers were caught and brought before the courts with ensuing heavy fines. These deterrents seemed to have little effect on what was undoubtedly a lucrative trade. For me, the luxury I missed most was ice cream and some time after the war, Mr Jackson at the Post Office produced rather a poor substitute to fill the demand. I remember well the taste of my first real ice cream some years later, probably 1948 – a delicious creamy Walls.

I used to look forward to bake day when Mum would bake loaves, teacakes and buns. She always put the dough on a long board immediately in front of the coal fire to get it to rise. The aroma, which is still with me today, and the cosiness of the warm kitchen are delightful memories. The best bit for me was getting the scrapes – my assiduous attention to every mixing bowl ensured these didn't need much effort to wash up. Mum did all the cooking in the coal oven and water was boiled in a cast iron kettle on a hinged griddle above the fire.

Sweets too didn't come off ration until 1952 and prior to this we made do with chewing liquorice root until it ended up a tasteless, stringy, woody mass. Food production became an all-consuming necessity and it seemed that every square inch of spare ground was turned over to vegetables and fruit. Most established gardens became devoid of flowers as their owners concentrated entirely on edible produce. Bottling and pickling seemed to become a home industry in itself. Domestic freezers were a thing of the future and I can't recall any household with a fridge. A capacious cold underground cellar was indeed a boon in any house and many of the older houses and cottages benefited immensely from this feature. In any event, most houses in the district did not have electricity to power domestic appliances and Scissett, in particular, had to rely on gas supplied by Norton's gasworks for lighting – few houses had gas cookers at this time. Farms and hamlets remote from the village didn't even have the benefit of piped gas and used paraffin oil lamps for lighting.

Clothing and footwear were also strictly rationed and new items could only be obtained with clothing coupons. Once again, housewives turned their talents to dressmaking and altering existing clothes to suit a potential new wearer. All items of children's clothing and shoes were passed down the family – the unlucky ones being the younger ones at the bottom of the chain. Eventually when clothes were no longer serviceable they were cut up into short strips and recycled to make pegged rugs. Knitting assumed the importance of a cottage industry and boys and girls turned up at school with home knitted jumpers, scarves, socks and gloves. Amazing as it may seem now, I was even taught to knit in junior school, although my efforts never progressed beyond dishcloths and those I did complete contained many unscheduled holes where I'd dropped a stitch. New shoes were particularly hard to come by and many pairs saw repairs upon repairs. As boys, we always wore heavy hob nailed boots to go to school since these were long lasting. They were ideal for sliding in the school yard, which produced a huge flurry of sparks as the iron nails in the boot soles and the heel irons struck the tarmac.

It was not only items on ration which were in short supply, but everyday goods disappeared from the shops. Metal, leather and rubber products in particular were like gold dust as the war effort had a vast appetite for these raw materials for the production of desperately needed weapons and munitions. An attitude of *make do and mend* rapidly took hold and people with no particular previous talent became experts in soldering, gluing and riveting in order to preserve and repair defective everyday articles, which in today's society would be immediately binned. Aluminium items, in particular, disappeared from the shops almost immediately in the cause of aeroplane production. It was possible to buy cork repair kits for holed aluminium pans and enamelled bowls and jugs, many of these makeshift repairs lasting well into post war times. Iron railings and gates were requisitioned, although many of the latter magically re-appeared at the end of the war, their owners obviously having decided that their contribution of a few pounds of wrought iron to the war effort would hardly defeat the Wehrmacht.

The war also delayed, until 1946, Norton's promised modernisation of our small rented house, known as a 'two up and two down' on account of it having just two downstairs rooms (a kitchen and a sitting room) and two bedrooms upstairs. The house, I guess, was built at the beginning of the 19th century and if it had been possible for someone from that era to visit, the main clues that things had moved forward a century or so would have been the sight of more modern furniture and a battery powered wireless. We didn't even have hot water 'on tap' but obtained it by ladling it from the boiler of the cast iron coal range – the ladle, incidentally, was always referred to by the dialect word *piggin*.

The lack of a hot water system meant that a bathroom was out of the question. Friday evening was always my bath night and immersion in the portable zinc bath's warm water in front of a roaring coal fire was a very pleasant experience. In complete contrast, and altogether unpleasant, was a visit to the earth closet situated in the yard at the back of the house, a walk of some 30 metres – a sore trial for a youngster walking in several inches of snow with the blizzard still blowing hard.

Illumination in the house was limited to a single gas mantle fitting in the kitchen screwed to a ceiling beam and a similar device in the sitting room. I was forbidden from attempting to light these with the usual wax taper until I was about 8 years old since the mantles were extremely fragile and easily damaged. We had no gas lighting in the bedrooms and bedtime saw me climbing the stairs with a lighted candle. In my bedroom, placed on the tiny dressing table, I had a small paraffin lamp, always known as a *curly lamp,* which gave out a comforting pale yellow light. On one occasion the wick must not have been trimmed correctly and my room was filled with smoke and the ceiling blackened with soot, much to Mum and Dad's consternation.

Information posters and slogans became a regular feature throughout the war and covered all manner of subjects. Spies were a number one priority and poster campaigns such as *Walls Have Ears* and *Loose Talk Costs Lives* were probably the most memorable. Clearly, information did reach the German propaganda machine and it must have been disconcerting for locals to hear Lord Haw Haw (William Joyce hanged for treason after the war) broadcasting from Germany details of everyday events, which were taking place in a particular district. It was not simply a war fought in the conventional sense, but it had for the first time a significant psychological dimension aimed at the civilian population.

Scissett was in an area much too hilly for airfields and about as far from the sea as it was possible to get. It was only natural, therefore, that the army presence dominated the area. The nearest barracks were at Kirkburton, some 5 miles from Scissett, whilst the grounds of Cannon Hall about 3 miles away were occupied by troops also. On Wheatley Hill, under a mile from my home, a searchlight battery was located. Even though I was only young at the start of the war, I remember conversations discussing which young men had been called up to serve in the forces. Uncle Colin was unlucky enough to receive an early call up, I believe, at the end of 1939 or early 1940. He was in the Royal Artillery, and after training was posted to Folkestone and Dover. First he saw service in the crew of a heavy gun battery blasting shells across the Channel, the main effect, I think, simply annoyed the enemy. The Germans, naturally, retaliated and the Kent coast was not a place for quiet relaxation. Ossie (from Shropshire I believe), uncle Colin's best mate in the army, was unlucky enough to be off-duty in the centre of Folkestone when a German shell landed and he was killed outright.

Later uncle Colin was promoted to lance corporal in command of a Lewis Gun Battery located in an exposed position on the jetty of Folkestone harbour, where the crew distinguished itself by shooting down an enemy plane. For uncle Colin to come home on leave was a rare treat for me. He invariably arrived home in uniform and always brought his 303 Enfield rifle. I amused myself for hours wearing his forage cap and lying on the settee with his rifle supported on the settee arm firing at an invisible enemy. On one occasion I contrived to trap my thumb in the rifle's breach resulting in a blackened nail. As I was now a casualty of war, Mum immediately forbade this activity, at least for the time being. Uncle Colin was one of the first to be demobbed, shortly after VE (Victory in Europe) Day, the rule of *first in, first out* operated in the conscripted army. I was overjoyed at his return.

Not all who left the village to fight were as lucky as uncle Colin. Looking at the names on Scissett's War Memorial I realised later that quite a few young men from the village didn't survive the war. However, the only one I can remember being killed was Peter Robinson. I knew him since he lived in Rock Villa, only 150 yards from my home. There were two Robinson families in Rock Villa and Peter was the son of Henry, who was a stoker in Norton's gas works. I believe that Peter was killed in a Beaufort night fighter in which he was a WOPAG (wireless operator/air gunner). I don't know whether this was through enemy action or whether it was some other unfortunate accident.

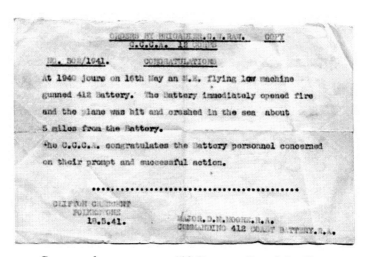

No. 505/1941. CONGRATULATIONS

At 1940 jours on 16th May an M.E. flying low machine gunned 412 Battery. The Battery immediately opened fire and the plane was hit and crashed in the sea about 5 miles from the Battery.

The C.C.C.A. congratulates the Battery personnel concerned on their prompt and successful action.

••

CLIFTON CRESCENT
FOLKESTONE
16.5.41.

MAJOR.D.M.MOORE.R.A.
COMMANDING 412 COAST BATTERY.R.A.

Congratulatory note to 412 Battery, Royal Artillery, Folkstone, 1941
Uncle Colin Bedford was a member of this Battery,
which successfully shot down an attacking German ME aircraft

Both the Home Guard and the Air Raid Warden organisations played an active role in the district during the war. The former group, as the name suggests, were an armed unit under the direct control of the army. They often carried out military exercises in the district, mainly based around Toppit and Wheatley Hill areas. The training exercises were carried out during the weekday evenings, on Saturday afternoon and on Sunday. Several times whilst out walking I was caught up in a cacophony of rifle and machine gun fire, fortunately for me blank ammunition was the order of the day. On one occasion I experienced, at close range, a thunderflash being let off in the plantation adjacent to the road up Wheatley Hill. There was a hell of a bang, which nearly made me jump out of my skin as it was totally unexpected. On other occasions I saw clay bombs being ignited and thrown for practice in the field on Scissett Common, where the unit had its ammunition store. Clay bombs, incidentally, simulated hand grenades, which were obviously far too dangerous to use in practice situations.

Air Raid Wardens took a less active role, but they still played an important part during and after raids. One of their tasks was to train the population to deal with incendiary bombs – sand, long scoops and stirrup pumps being the main counter measures. Stirrup pumps were issued to selected households. Our next-door neighbour but one, Mr Hughes, took charge of the pump allocated to our row of four houses. Another of the Wardens' tasks was to report unexploded bombs to the authorities. My future father-in-law, Herbert Fox, who held the position of Chief Air Raid Warden in Emley, often recounted, with a wry smile, the story of his failure to report an unexploded bomb, which had fallen in a field in Tyburn Lane only some 20 yards from his home. Apparently, when the authorities discovered his omission and the bomb disposal squad had removed the offending ordnance, he received a severe reprimand and the threat of demotion hung over him for the rest of the war – for the latter, he was not in the least bit concerned.

From time to time realistic exercises were carried out in the disused Cuttlehurst Mill, some 100 yards from my home. This was a substantial 5 storey stone building with all its wooden floors intact and was an ideal site to practice rescue operations. I delighted in watching the antics of the various organisations, including the fire brigade and ambulance crews. From what I could judge, the whole exercise seemed an excellent simulation of a bomb-hit building with fires being lit on various floors and smoke bombs and explosions adding to the general mayhem.

Like most boys of my age, I soon became familiar with the technology of warfare. I became expert in recognising the silhouettes of our own and enemy aircraft. Guns, such as the Bren, Lewis and Sten held no mystery and I could easily identify the various rounds of ammunition. It was surprising how many live rounds were in circulation, even amongst us boys, and I can remember, late in the war, letting off a 303 round by wedging it in a stone wall on Scissett Common and administering a sharp hammer blow to a nail held against the detonator. As boys, we collected bits of military hardware and there was a thriving swaps market. German pieces were always highly prized and amongst my collection I boasted several chunks from a downed Heinkel bomber as well as a dozen or so spent cartridge cases from German cannon and machine guns, which had fallen from the sky during aerial combat. Each year there were fund raising efforts such as Warships Week and Wings for Victory Week. During these events, exhibitions and demonstrations of military hardware were held in Scissett Parish Room, which I avidly attended every night throughout the week. Tanks regularly rumbled through Scissett on their test runs. This vital activity rendered the tarmac surface of the A636 almost into a ploughed field and provided continuous employment for the council repair gang. The tanks were manufactured in Wakefield at the British Jeffery Diamond (BJD) works.

As the war progressed, German aerial activity decreased and nightly visits to the air raid shelter became a thing of the past. However, Hitler decided to liven up my Christmas 1944 by sending a V1 flying bomb to disturb the district. I was lying awake in bed that Christmas Eve, wondering what presents lay in store for me the following morning. Then, in the distance I heard a faint pulsating noise, which gradually got louder until it appeared to be directly overhead. I'd never heard a deafening sound remotely like this and I conjectured that it was a low flying heavy bomber in distress. Shortly after the noise had died away I heard a faint muffled explosion, which I assumed to be the bomber crashing. Later I learnt that it was a doodle bug (the common nickname for a V1 flying bomb), which had come down in a field at Grange Moor, some 5 miles away. Many years later, I read that this wayward intruder was one of about 20 V1s, which had been launched from German bombers out over the North Sea, the cities of Manchester and Liverpool being the intended targets. An exciting close to the year occurred just one week later, on New Years Eve, when I experienced quite a severe (by local standards) earthquake. Studying geology at University many years later, I learnt that this was due to movement on the South Craven fault in North Yorkshire.

During my time in the junior school, I encountered children who didn't speak in the local dialect as I did. These were the evacuees from London and the Southeast who had been moved to the district to escape the heavy bombing in those parts. I felt very sorry for these boys and girls, some as young as 5 years old, who had been separated from their parents. The evacuees were a resilient lot and soon integrated into school and village life. For my part, I just hoped the German attacks on us didn't increase, for I dreaded the thought of being sent away from Mum – in the event, there was little likelihood of that happening, although I didn't know it at the time. Miss Norton from Bagden Hall was the leading light in arranging accommodation for the evacuees and set an example by taking in one of her own. The girl's name was Barbara Butler, who, like several in the district, never returned to her family after the war. Barbara attended Scissett School before gaining entry to Wakefield Girls High School and I believe that Miss Norton formally adopted her.

As a schoolboy, I was fully aware of the war's progress – initially there seemed to be nothing but defeats and set-backs. I often wondered how long it would all last and gradually as my pre-war memories receded, wartime simply became the norm. The Allies, by 1943 were beginning to score significant victories on land, sea and in the air and I somehow sensed that in the end the Axis powers would be defeated.

Radio bulletins, newspapers, and cinema newsreels were the main sources of information. I remember hearing the news bulletin of the daring and successful Dambusters Raid on the Moehne, Eder and Sorpe Dams during the night of 16th/17th May 1943 and the tremendous excitement that this caused in school. Similar excitement occurred when the Allied landings had been made in Normandy on 6th June 1944. The newspapers gave first hand accounts of operations in the various theatres of war, usually accompanied by photographs and maps of the action. Weekly Pathe newsreels, in black and white, were shown in cinemas and brought together the home front and the war front. Mum or auntie May often took me to the Savoy cinema in Skelmanthorpe for the Saturday matinee or the first house in the evening. Information released to the general public in films, news bulletins and newspapers was always censored and specific locations and place names were hardly ever revealed. In school, maps were put up on the wall showing the progress of the war. Consequently, the names and locations of European towns, cities and rivers soon became familiar.

Many years later during the Cold War, I had the thrill of crossing the Rivers Oder and Neisse several times. For me these rivers had attained almost mystical significance as the post-war boundary between Poland and East Germany, both of these countries up to 1989 being part of the Communist Eastern Block. To us boys, the names of military commanders, Eisenhower, Montgomery, Patton in the west and Zhukov, Rokossowsky, Konev in the east, tripped off the tongue. They were indeed heroes and induced a cult following, possibly greater than football stars of today.

In school we followed the relentless progress of the Allied forces through France and on into Germany as well as the Russian army, which was driving west towards Berlin. I sensed even as early as the breakout from Normandy that we were now certain to win, a view reinforced by the crushing defeat of the Germans in the Falaise Pocket. Here the mighty 5th Panzer and 7th Army were virtually annihilated with the loss of over 50,000 men and all their equipment. Basking in the sun, sipping a coffee outside a café in the lovely square in Falaise exactly 60 years later, it was almost impossible for me to comprehend the carnage, which must have occurred in this now pleasant and tranquil spot.

After such a resounding defeat I was amazed just how resilient and tenacious the German defence would be. The improbable German counter attack in the Ardennes at the end of 1944 certainly gave the advancing allied armies a nasty jolt, but even with that set back I still felt confident of the ultimate outcome. Once the Rhine had been crossed and the fighting was on German soil, the defence became desperate as young and old were thrown into battle. I heard reports of young boys from the Hitler Jugend (Hitler Youth) fighting alongside the regulars and handling panzerfausts (anti tank rockets) with considerable skill. I thought at the time just how brave these young lads were and also how desperate the Germans had become to sacrifice lives not much older than mine.

The war in Europe came to an end on the 7th May 1945 with the unconditional surrender of all German forces to the Allies. The next day was designated VE (Victory in Europe) Day and I was delighted to have the day off school, which I spent helping to build a huge celebration bonfire on the Pit Hill overlooking the village. The bonfire was lit after dark a few days later, but some of the wood was pretty damp and it took a few cans of paraffin to induce a decent level of combustibility. Some members of the Home Guard enlivened proceedings by letting off thunderflashes, smoke bombs and clay bombs. I can remember my feelings at this time were of great relief and tremendous joy that the conflict in Europe was now ended. The savage war in the Far East was still being waged and although many British troops were involved, this theatre of war never seemed to assume the importance of the European conflict – on reflection, because it didn't pose a direct threat to the country. The Second World War, the world's greatest conflict, finally ended on 2nd September 1945, six years and one day after Germany invaded Poland. The total cost in human life lost can only be estimated at tens of millions, the cost in human suffering inestimable.

I lived through these terrible times, but for me, as a boy, these were exciting times. Back in 1945, with the war now ended, I knew that my life would be altered radically, but I really had no idea what changes would lie ahead. This was simply because, in reality, I'd never known anything but war, my peacetime pre-war memories having faded dramatically, almost beyond recall. If I had ever imagined that things, such as the restoration of street lighting, the end of rationing and other war strictures would change overnight, I was sadly disappointed. The country, in fact, returned to normality only very slowly with some wartime measures lasting for years. If I had been born just a few years earlier I would certainly have been called up to fight. Who knows what fate would have had in store for me? Lucky or what?

7

THE KNOWLEDGE

My introduction to the English education system was anything but auspicious. I must have been just over 4 years old when, on one occasion, Mum walked me into the village centre. As we approached the Co-op butchers we were met by a long crescendo of noise, which would have done Rossini proud, except it wasn't tuneful. Mum lifted me up to look over a low stone wall alongside the butchers. I was horror struck. What appeared to me to be utter mayhem was in reality nothing more than little tots running round aimlessly like demented ants and creating a dreadful cacophony of sound. Mum explained that this was playtime at Scissett Infants School and that before too long I would be joining in. Fear struck me immediately and from that time on I truly did dread the inevitable first school day, although I did my utmost not to think about it too much.

My adventure in the English education system began in September 1940, when I was a rising 5 year old. By this time the Infants school in the village centre had closed and all children up to 11 years old were now taught in the Junior school at the foot of Scissett Common. To say that I hated going to school in the early weeks was an understatement. It was far more than that - I feared it. I didn't dislike the work, the routine or the teachers. It was because I felt overwhelmed and alienated in, what seemed to me, an enormous group of children. I found it difficult to join in the little cliques, which youngsters only 5 years old had formed, and I was very shy making the initial approach. I suppose this is understandable because I was an only child and much of my time at home had been spent alone or in the company of just one or two playmates.

During the early weeks, Mum and the teachers had an anxious time keeping me from running away. My favoured time of escape was right at the start of the day. Mum walked me to school and I would hang about near the gate watching until she disappeared from sight. This was my cue to slip away. I'd follow her back over Scissett Common dodging down behind the wall from time to time until I could cut across the Pit Hill and make my way down to grandma Bedford's. There I would hide in the ashpit of the earth closet until I was confident I wouldn't be returned back to school that same morning. I reckon grandma had a bad time at school too, because she was always sympathetic. Invariably she sat me in front of the lovely warm coal fire and plied me with tea and buns. As far as I know, she never betrayed our secret to Mum. Although there was nothing physically wrong with me, I truly did suffer tummy pains – just a bad attack of nerves I suppose.

Gradually I gained more confidence and by the half term holiday I'd settled into a reasonable routine. Mrs Taylor was the infants' teacher and she had a kind, but at the same time, firm manner and there wasn't much that we little urchins could get away with. Sadness came some 18 months later when Mrs Taylor retired. I can't remember the name of the teacher who replaced her since she only taught me for the final few months of my spell in the infants. She was, like Mrs Taylor, a very kind, gentle person. My educational progress in infants was sound without being brilliant. Using a pencil, I learnt to write detached letters, both upper and lower case, which we called printing. We were encouraged to write small sentences and to use elementary punctuation – I found it immensely satisfying to put a huge dot for the full stop at the end of a sentence. My reading ability was pretty good since I had books at home and often read to Mum for half an hour or so each evening. Number work was mainly confined to addition and subtraction.

The war, which had broken out a year before I started school, had an immense influence on our daily routine. We were required to carry gas masks to school each day and to keep them with us under our desks during class. The gas masks were supplied in a stout brown cardboard box and most Mums produced a fabric cover with a decent wide strap to go around the neck. The original 'strap' was just rough brown string and soreness soon developed at the back of the neck after walking only a short distance. All of us feared the arrival at school of the 'gas van', a frightening experience for 5 year olds. This large, dark, forbidding van was parked in the schoolyard and we had to line up wearing our gas masks before climbing the couple or so steps into the van's dimly lit interior. Doors were then tightly closed and we were incarcerated for about 10 minutes in an atmosphere, which I now assume was tear gas. It was a blessed relief to be let out and the officials then checked each of us in turn for signs of running eyes. Those who were unlucky enough to display the symptoms had their gas masks adjusted and were required to repeat the ordeal.

Air raid practices featured frequently in school life at this time. The school bell was rung and each class teacher then blew her whistle as the signal for us to don our gas masks and take shelter under our desks. This was an exciting event and was accompanied by loud drumming of heels on the wooden floor, much to Mrs Taylor's annoyance. The greatest danger was not from German bombs, but from the floor splinters, which on every occasion seemed to find the tender part of at least one pupil's anatomy. After the initial excitement of the under-desk scramble had subsided, a deathly hush ensued and we strained our ears for the faintest sound of approaching enemy bombers. Many hopefuls amongst us claimed to have heard them, but no lone raider ever materialised, let alone a massed formation.

Growing up before and during the war meant that I, along with everyone else, did not have the benefit of the National Health Service (NHS), which was founded by the post war Labour Government in 1946. All visits to the doctor, in my case to Doctor Mommen's Surgery at Park Mill, Clayton West, resulted in a bill for the consultation as well as for treatment and medicines. One of the earliest visits to his surgery I remember was for injections against Diphtheria, which in those days was quite common and something of a killer. Epidemics of the usual childhood ailments, Whooping Cough, German Measles, Chicken Pox and Measles swept through the school regularly and decimated attendances. Fortunately, I was a healthy lad and the only really severe illness I had was Measles, which necessitated the Doctor visiting me at home daily for a whole week.

In view of the onerous health costs to working families, it's no surprise that some weird and wonderful home treatments had been devised. One, which still amuses me today, is the belief that a brown paper shirt lavishly spread with goose grease and worn next to the chest could ward off colds and infections. One can well imagine the smell, which greeted teachers when a whole class wore this apparel for the duration of winter. Norton's gas works was the scene of one of the most bizarre and vicious treatments I was subjected to. At the first sign of a cold or cough, Mum would walk me there and have a word with the shift stoker, often Henry Robinson. He would then open the small inspection cover on top of one of the scrubbers and I'd have to stick my nose in and take several deep breaths. The potent mixture of coal gas, oxides of nitrogen and sulphur and the noxious vapours of the benzene family certainly cleared the tubes – probably damaged the lining too if the truth were known!

After my allotted 2 years in the infants I was then moved up to the middle school class to be taught, or more like terrorised, by the doughty Miss Smith. She was, I suppose, about 60 years old and had taught most of the parents of those currently in my class. She had a sharp tongue and had no qualms about visiting the sins of fathers (and mothers) upon the children. My parents must have been pretty good for never once did she shout at me "you're as stupid as your dad." In the case of the girls it was always "you're as stupid as your mother." In her class we sat in individual desks with isles between each row. Like a hawk she patrolled the room and anyone who she deemed to be slacking received a sharp painful prod in the back with the wooden foot ruler she always carried. As she moved around the classroom she would examine the progress of our written work and any mistake was punished with quite a vicious slap across the wrist and back of the hand with the foot ruler. I suppose I was one of the lucky ones, for, although my efforts were not always perfect, I was nevertheless pretty sharp and a reasonably quick, tidy worker. I was thus able to maintain a low profile and avoid the worst of her tirades. I have some sympathy for her since she had to teach children of wide ranging ability spanning 2 academic years, the class size, I suppose, being around the 40 mark – quite a handful. For her to keep all of us occupied and out of mischief was quite a feat. However, I felt very sorry for the slower ones in the class who had a continual struggle to keep up – she never attempted 'setting' into ability groups and in consequence the less bright ones, if they couldn't grasp something, fell further and further behind.

During my second year in Miss Smith's class I was appointed an ink monitor. This was a desirable and coveted position since the duties took the post holder out of the classroom for twenty minutes or so on Monday mornings and again on Friday afternoons. The Monday duty involved making the ink up from ink powder using water obtained in the boys' cloakroom. The chore was then completed by returning to the classroom and filling each desk inkwell with the product. The Friday duty was simply collecting the inkwells and emptying out any ink remaining, finally washing out each inkwell ready for the following week. In Miss Smith's class we progressed to writing with a dip pen, which really was an art. Many times, the steel nib at the end of a plain wooden handle mysteriously got 'crossed' and, more often than not in these circumstances, attempts at forming letters ended up with ink drops being splattered all over the page. By the time I was moved to the top class I was able to do decent 'joined up' writing and my ability at reading and arithmetic certainly placed me in the top ten percent of my year. I was somewhat relieved to be promoted from Miss Smith's class to join the 'top' class two terms earlier than my age dictated.

The school's headmistress and teacher of the 'top' class, when I arrived in it, was Miss Leng. She was an austere woman, who always seemed to be dressed in brown. I honestly believe she had

Scissett Infants School, circa 1908, my mother 4th from left, back row of girls

Scissett School class, circa 1910. My father standing middle back row

no ambition for her charges, but viewed us merely as mines and mills fodder. I hope that my judgement is not too harsh, but even after some 60 years that's how it still seems. The school hadn't much of an academic track record, measured by its success of getting children into grammar school, but of course the 1944 Education Act hadn't been long enacted when I reached the top class.

A profound and dramatic change took place with the arrival of Miss Pears as the new head. She was a brilliant teacher who lifted our eyes above the horizon and made us feel we could achieve our full potential. I was so impressed when she brought her own copy of Pears Encyclopaedia into school for us to consult on our own – for some time I firmly believed that she had written it! She moved into the school house in Springfield Avenue with her father, who provided her with considerable help in school by doing odd jobs and taking the gardening class. Of course, there were food shortages and the school garden provided a decent supply of fruit and vegetables, which were sold to Mums with the proceeds going to school funds.

Miss Pears set about reorganising the teaching schedule in the top class and this move benefited me enormously. Mornings were allocated to academic work whilst the afternoons, although hardly play, were set aside for projects and 'recreational' learning. I was lucky in being selected to join the group deemed to be potential grammar school material (the scholarship group), numbering 7 out of a class of about 35. The morning's teaching was devoted entirely to mathematics (mainly arithmetic) and English, which included spelling, reading, essay writing (known as composition) and punctuation. For the scholarship group alone, practice in the intelligence test (a feature of the 11 plus grammar school entrance examination) was an every day routine. Each morning commenced with the whole class being drilled in multiplication tables. First, we chanted out-loud a selection of tables, up to and including the 12 times table. Indeed, even today, I can still hear the sing-song intonation of 35 childish voices belting out 1 times 2 is 2, 2 times 2 is 4 and so on. Then came the individual oral tests. Miss Pears stood at the front of the class and systematically went round firing a multiplication question at each pupil in turn. I was lucky in having a decent memory and these tests held no fears. Eventually, those who she deemed to know the tables were excused, in order that she could concentrate on the remainder. I felt quite superior to be on the 'excused tables' list.

For the rest of the morning, the class was essentially taught in two groups. First, she would give the scholarship group a piece of prose to read quietly, which would then form the basis of the comprehension test later in the morning. During this time she would be involved with the remainder in the class who were working at a slower pace. She would then return to work with the scholarship group for the rest of the morning, only going back occasionally to oversee the work of the remainder. I certainly benefited enormously from this intensive coaching. Mathematics was confined to arithmetic and associated problems and by the time the 11 plus exam arrived we were all very competent in the 4 rules – addition, subtraction, long multiplication and long division. In addition we could handle fractions and decimals and also quite complex problems. These were, of course, pre-decimalisation days and the old weights and measures systems really tested 10 and 11 year olds' mathematical ability. Taking weights in the Avoirdupois System as an example, addition, subtraction, multiplication or division of, say, 19 tons, 15 hundredweights, 3 quarters, 1 stone, 13 pounds, 14 ounces first of all required knowledge of the weights table:

16 ounces = 1 pound
14 pounds = 1 stone
2 stones = 1 quarter
4 quarters = 1 hundredweight
20 hundredweights = 1 ton

It was also useful, at times, to remember that there are 28 pounds in a quarter, 112 pounds in one hundredweight and 2240 pounds in a ton.

Referring to the above problem, it can be seen that we had to use no less than 5 different number bases, although we never recognised it as such at the time. Forty years later, with the advent of computers, the school mathematics curriculum introduced work in one base only (base 2), which was considered a difficult topic. Really!! There were also similar difficulties with Imperial units of length and volume. The *inch, foot, yard, chain, furlong* and *mile* were the basic elements of length, the multiples in this case being 12, 3, 22, 10 and 8. Volumes were measured in *gills, pints, quarts* and *gallons*, the multiples in this case being 2 or 4, depending on the liquid being measured. Such complexity really does make the metric system, where the multiples are always 10, look rather easy. 1971 saw the change from *pounds, shillings* and *pence* (£-s-d), a monetary system in which there were 20 shillings in £1 and 12 pence in a shilling to a much simpler system in which the shilling was eliminated and there are 100 new pence in £1.

Of course, it wasn't only the 3 R's, which occupied our time. Miss Pears taught history in a very systematic manner, although, in truth there were long periods of our history of which I was totally oblivious. This is understandable, for it is hard to cover something like 2000 plus years in any depth. My favourite topics were the Romans and the Normans, because both appeared to be such a powerful lot and pretty organised with it. The Wars of the Roses was another major topic, although it was only years later that I figured out it wasn't simply my Yorkshire lads warring with those living in Lancashire. It never struck me as odd at the time that apart from the battles of Wakefield (1460) and Towton (1461) none of the remaining battles, skirmishes and confrontations took place in the two counties. The Civil War too made quite an impact on me and in those days I was firmly on the side of the Royalists – Oliver Cromwell, I reckoned, was far too much of a spoil sport!

I loved geography too, learning about different continents and countries overseas. The syllabus was, of course, factually based, learning names of capitals, rivers, mountain ranges and the like,

We studied Great Britain too and Yorkshire in particular. The major rivers of Yorkshire from north to south, *S*wale, *U*re, *N*idd, *W*harfe, *A*ire and *D*on, I still remember from the memory jogger, *Sunwad*. I was more than pleased to learn that Yorkshire was not only the largest county, but was responsible for at least one tenth of all the country's products, coal, textiles, agricultural produce etc. No wonder Yorkshire folk tend to feel like the Texans in America, that is, very superior.

It wasn't all hard classroom slog and the highlight of the year was the annual school outing to York with the obligatory halt at Towton to see the site of the Yorkist rout of the Lancastrian army. There, I learnt, that on Palm Sunday 1461 some 10,000 Yorkist archers, aided by a strong following wind and a heavy snowstorm, commenced the slaughter of the Lancastrian forces. In a macabre way, we revelled in the fact that some 20,000 Lancastrians met their end and the River Cock that day, reportedly, ran red with blood. Some 8,000 Yorkists also perished, which made the fatalities the highest of any battle fought on British soil. It has also been calculated that at least 0.8% of the whole English population were killed or wounded in that one day - a reflection of the terrible carnage.

Nature study provided light relief too and the afternoon nature walks into the Duke Wood and down Stoney Lane were a welcome break from the classroom. I must confess, however, that to me it seemed rather a girly pursuit and I couldn't be bothered to remember the names of plants and flowers – something, which the girls seemed to excel at. The school had quite a large garden and there the gardening class was taken by Miss Pears's father. Again, we viewed this activity as a welcome relief from the classroom and something we quite enjoyed.

The school was a substantial stone building with very high pointed slate roofs. It dated back to the mid Victorian period and featured large gothic windows and high ceilings. Consequently it was a cold draughty place especially in winter. The central heating system relied on a coke-fired boiler located underneath the room used by the top class and reached by steps down from the girls' playground. The heating pipes, which served each classroom were about 8 inches diameter to allow water circulation by convection only, electric circulatory pumps being a thing of the future. After the weekend, the heating pipes warmed only slowly and in winter it was probably Monday afternoon before the school reached a tolerable temperature and we could take off our outdoor coats. The boiler, had the habit, from time to time, of dosing the classroom above with acrid fumes and, in retrospect, it's a miracle we didn't suffer carbon monoxide poisoning.

The winter months were particularly hard during the 1940's and visits to the unheated outside toilets was something of a torture – the boys' urinal didn't even have a roof. Of course, ice formed regularly in the toilet bowls and the girls must have endured considerable discomfort. All boys in those days wore short trousers, even in the depths of winter, and our knees became extremely sore and red (the skin often breaking) as the snow or wind blasted into the bare flesh above the tops our woollen knee-socks and below the short trouser legs.

The winter of 1947 was, according to official records, the most severe of the 20th century, certainly the worst I can ever remember. Deep snow covered the ground from just after mid January, through the whole of February and for much of March. Rarely did the temperature rise above freezing even at mid-day. I felt cheated that I did not attend one of several local schools, which from time to time, were forced to close. The school's central heating system hadn't been designed to cope with such sustained low temperatures, consequently we spent much of the time indoors still wrapped up in outdoor clothing. We still took our morning and afternoon playtimes outdoors and had the satisfaction of constructing a massive snow igloo in the boys' playground since football and other games had, obviously, to be suspended.

As a group, we were a lively bunch and playtimes for the boys invariably involved physical activity. When I first started school there seemed to be many playtime fights amongst the boys, but by the time I reached the top class things had quietened down considerably. The boys occupied the playground on the south side of the school alongside Lower Common Road, whilst the girls used the playground on the school's north side, adjacent to Barnsley Road. Miss Pears, despite being a spinster, was certainly enlightened and did her bit for social awareness by allowing the boys and girls in the top class to mix and use the boys' playground. Previously, social contact between the sexes at playtime had been strictly prohibited.

In winter, the boys always played football, with the goals marked in chalk on the walls at each end of the playground or coats dropped on the floor. The wall on the west side of the playground was none too high and any lofted shots at goal ended up with the ball in Victor Senior's field. Victor must have complained about our intrusions for we were not supposed to climb the wall to retrieve the ball. The teachers knew full well that was precisely what we were doing and usually turned a blind eye to this minor misdemeanour. The playing surface was tarmac and enthusiastic tackles usually resulted in scraped knees, arms and elbows as the unfortunate recipient hit the deck. Looking back, I'm amazed no one broke a leg or an arm. In summer, cricket was the favoured game, although we always used a tennis ball or a rubber ball. Even then, the large windows of the infants' classroom were rattled with astonishing regularity and for them to survive intact was nothing short of a miracle.

There were minor welfare provisions in school. A teaspoonful of cod liver oil was sold for a farthing, I believe. Milk was supplied in $^1/_3$ pint glass bottles and one bottle was available without charge to every pupil at morning playtime. In winter, the milk was often delivered in a frozen state and we resorted to thawing the bottles' contents on the central heating pipes.

One welfare service, which struck fear into all our hearts was the periodic visit of the school dentist, Mr. Mackay, a dour Scot who showed us no mercy. He set up his temporary surgery in a small room off the top classroom and the dentist's chair was an austere wooden job with no arms. His drill was a simple affair powered by a foot treadle and the pain he inflicted with this device was nothing short of excruciating. For the drilling process, anaesthetic injections were never offered – from my limited experience of their use for the odd extraction at the time, they were unpleasant anyway and the numbing effect on the face seemed to last for hours. From then onward until just a few years ago, I refused all injections for fillings and extractions and on one occasion I even had a nerve removed without anaesthetic – a hangover from those primitive days.

Cooked school dinners were introduced in the mid 1940's, which were a tremendous benefit to the pupils from the outlying farms, who previously had to bring a packed lunch. I believe the cost was 5 old pence per dinner, equivalent to just over 2 pence in today's currency. The schools in the district did not have individual kitchens, but the meals were cooked in a central kitchen situated on Kaye Line in Denby Dale. The hot meals, in insulated metal containers, were then transported by lorry to each school. The older boys had to help with carrying the full containers into school and returning the previous day's empties back to the lorry. Our school was the penultimate delivery point, with Clayton West school the final drop-off. On several occasions my mates and myself decided to temporarily bunk off school and hitch a ride in the lorry to Clayton West and back. I suppose that we would be absent for about 15 minutes and I'm surprised it took Miss Pears so long to discover our ruse. A good telling off ensued!

In view of the dominance of the Norton family, who clearly eschewed any nonconformist activity in 'their' village, the school was a Church of England (C of E) establishment, in contrast to the Board schools of neighbouring villages, where, in general, the chapels held sway. Lest it be thought that religious, in particular, Anglican indoctrination was high on the agenda, this was certainly not the case. All schools were compelled by law to hold an assembly each morning set in a religious, that is, Christian context. In this regard, Scissett School was no different from any other, the assembly simply being a hymn (*Every morning the red sun rises warm and bright* being a favourite) followed by a reading and the notices. The only concession that I could see, which revealed any Anglican influence, was the regular Tuesday visit of the Vicar, Mr Legg. On that morning he took the assembly and afterwards spent about 10 minutes speaking to each of the 3 classes in turn. By no stretch of the imagination could that be called hard line Anglican indoctrination.

The 11 plus examination was held at the start of the second term for the 10/11 year old age group. In 1947, when I was due to sit, the exam was scheduled to take place in late January at Scissett Secondary Modern School. However, because entrants had to travel from schools situated some distance from the examination centre, the first deep snow of winter caused a postponement to a date in mid February. I geared myself up again for the exam on the revised date only to find that a second postponement was necessary as a result of a second huge snowfall (the previous one never having thawed anyway). Along with something like 60-70 other hopefuls, I finally turned up for the exam one day in March, snow still lying on the ground.

The exam consisted of 4 written papers; Arithmetic (including problems), English composition, a Comprehension test and an Intelligence test. The latter was also something of a speed test too. The paper had 100 questions of the type where one had to determine the next in a series of numbers or to spot the 'odd one out' in a group of almost identical shapes. Those candidates whose schools had not given them any, or sufficient, practice in this mysterious art were placed at a considerable disadvantage. I remember too the advice Miss Pears drummed into us that we should move on and not waste time racking our brains if we were unable to see the solution almost immediately. I followed this advice faithfully and reached the 96th question before time was called, having missed out on about 5. I figured that even if I'd got one or two incorrect, then I was still going to end up with a mark of over 80%. I knew too that I'd done pretty well on the arithmetic paper, as I had completed this and I'd had sufficient time to quickly check my answers. After the exam, I couldn't help thinking that my future education might well depend upon the subjective assessment of a written essay together with the more exact assessment of a comprehension test. In truth, I was fairly optimistic, but at the same time very afraid of failure.

The exam results were communicated by letter to the school and I awaited anxiously for that fateful day. Miss Pears had the good sense to call us individually into the small room off the main classroom to tell us our fate. I was truly overjoyed and mightily relieved that a grammar school was to be my future destiny. As a reward, we were allowed to go home and tell our parents the good news. In my case, Mum was at home to share my joy but Dad was, as usual, out at work. Mum rang him from the village phone box later that morning. I made the best of my good news by running down to Rock Villa and letting grandma Bedford and auntie May know before returning to school. Of the scholarship group, I was the only boy to pass, but amongst the girls, Dorothy Ellis, Marilyn Blackburn, Greta Batty and Audrey Calvert made it too.

The choice of Grammar School didn't pose a problem for Mum and Dad. They would not hear of me going to Holme Valley Grammar School at Honley as they considered this institution something of an inferior upstart, which only dated back to the 1930's. Furthermore, I think they were influenced by a saying, which had widespread currency in the district and referred to the Holme Valley's Red and Green colours: *Red and Green is seldom seen except on a gorbey's back,* gorbey being the local dialect word for an idiot. So, Penistone Grammar School would be my formal education world for the next few years.

School broke up in July for the long summer holiday and as I walked out onto Barnsley Road for the last time clutching my final school report, I felt very sad. Other than the first few weeks, I had been very happy indeed in the school, especially in the top class. Even as an 11 year old, I realised that a significant era of my life had ended. My final report showed what a demanding taskmistress Miss Pears really was. Despite achieving the maximum marks of $^{60}/_{60}$ for Arithmetic and $^{20}/_{20}$ for English Composition, her grading was only *Good* – not *Very Good* nor *Excellent* as one would one normally expect. I achieved the top position in the class and her final comment made me smile when I read the report some 60 years after it was written: *Edward is an intelligent boy, eager to learn. He well deserves his high position on the list.* Miss Pears not only taught me well, she gave me confidence and a love of learning (sadly, I didn't always work so hard in the next phase of my education journey). Truly, I could not have had a more inspiring teacher, who gave me a wonderful start in life. Once again, luck had been on my side.

8
Freedom

Without a shadow of doubt, man's greatest mechanical invention, after the wheel of course, was the humble bicycle. The most efficient means of transport ever devised and with it came freedom for the masses at the turn of the 19th century. So it was with me, some 50 years later. I was still in junior school and more than anything else in the world, it was a bike I craved. Anything, so long as it had 2 wheels. Most of my pals had one and I was beginning to feel distinctly underprivileged in this area of life. I can still remember the very day I learned to ride a two-wheeler, as we called them then. This experience, a youngster's equivalent of learning to fly, came to me in the yard adjacent to Hirst Buckley's printing works at the bottom of Bagden Lane. My pal, Garth, was a trusting (or possibly foolhardy) lad, for it was on his bike that I wobbled off on my first solo effort – truly a miracle I didn't fall off and buckle the wheels or inflict some other mortal damage to his pride and joy.

Mum and Dad had always said I could have a bike when I had learned to ride. Looking back, it seems a curious attitude for them to adopt - something akin to telling a potential mountaineer that he can have a pair of specialist climbing boots when he's conquered Everest. Anyway, my side of the bargain had been fulfilled and it was now up to them to deliver. They didn't disappoint! £6 changed hands and uncle Colin's bike, which had hung over the staircase at Rock Villa all through the war, passed to me. I was so proud. Rather than a rusty old ramshackle, many of which were around at that time, I'd taken possession of a virtually unused, shiny, black Dawes sports job with $26 \times 1^{3/}{}_{8}$ inch tyres, side pull cable brakes and best of all, a 3 speed wide ratio Sturmey Archer hub gear. Oh, I almost forgot - it came complete with a beautiful capacious black leather saddlebag.

That bike and its saddlebag transformed my life. Even before I'd left junior school I was able to ride for miles and in so doing push the limits of my known world to, what seemed, incredible distances in all directions. At first, I limited my explorations along the main roads to the towns of Huddersfield, Barnsley and Wakefield. Each of these centres of population was within 10 miles of home and the round trip could be easily accomplished in an afternoon. I never worried about going to places I hadn't visited before – in those happy days the thought of being abducted or of some other bloodthirsty crime against my person was furthest from my mind.

My worst fear, indeed dread, was for a punctured tyre. I was remarkably lucky, for I can remember it happening only once, and that fortunately occurred within pushing distance of home. It is true that I knew the theory of puncture repair, but I feared that my practical application might be found lacking. What worried me most of all was not removing the wheel or the offending tyre, but actually finding the tiny pinprick in the inner tube. I used to pray that, should I ever be unlucky enough to sustain a puncture, it would happen alongside a body of water – a river, a stream or a horse trough (yes, there were still quite a few still extant in those days). I would then have the resource to detect the telltale stream of bubbles pinpointing the air leak.

For a while, my excursions were confined mainly to the main roads, which in those days were remarkably traffic free and consequently almost without danger. One of my early forays off the main roads was in company with a group of friends from junior school to visit Tinker's Monument, a tower like structure situated on the moors high above Hepworth village at an elevation of over 1200 feet above sea level. For me, this stark and remote edifice had gained almost mystical qualities. Since early childhood, I had viewed it many times from various vantage points around Scissett, but its mystery never diminished. In the end, my curiosity could be contained no longer and I persuaded a group of my cycling friends from junior school that an unbroken climb of some 1000 feet, or so, with one or two pretty steep gradients, was going to be worth the effort. Several potential explorers owned heavy single gear roadster bikes more suited to a trip to the local shops, but they all agreed to the 20 mile round trip of quite difficult pedalling. Plans were duly laid, and at mid-morning on Easter Monday 1947 the expedition got under way.

We made rather slow progress and arrived at our goal, puffing, sweating and red faced, but with the enthusiasm of pilgrims arriving at Mecca. The building was a formidable and somewhat threatening looking structure, which the smoke, even high on the moors, had managed to turn jet black. It was built in mid Victorian times, and despite that generation's reputation for building sound engineering structures, it collapsed, sometime, I think, in the mid 1950's. Our biggest surprise however, was to find deep snow still lying on the ground from the very heavy falls which had occurred earlier in the winter. Despite the sun shining, it was bitterly cold when we ate our sandwiches. It was then I realised for the first time the dramatic effect that altitude and wind had on the temperature – an early experience of the wind chill factor, which in those days was never quantified nor even mentioned.

We were now in an area criss-crossed with a spider's web of minor unclassified roads. There were no signposts on these minor roads, since these had not yet been replaced, having been removed in 1939 to confuse German invaders. We were certainly confused and our subsequent journey took us in totally the wrong direction. We headed west into Lancashire and Cheshire, although at the time we were totally oblivious to our gross navigational error. It was an unpleasant shock to find a main road signpost at Saltersbrook, some 1600 feet above sea level, the highest point of the Woodhead Pass, on the A628 between Manchester and Sheffield. That was our turning point and from there we managed to find our way through Penistone and finally arrived home unharmed, but totally exhausted after a journey of something over 40 miles. It was not the distance, which had caused the spindly-legged ones amongst us the problem, but the amount of climbing on single gear bikes. With all the ups and downs I reckon we climbed something approaching the height of a minor mountain. The following morning I was so stiff I could hardly hobble and it was days before the aches left my body.

Getting lost on the Tinker's Monument expedition taught me a sharp lesson, but it didn't deter my desire to explore the bye ways. What I needed was a decent bit of navigational kit and what better than a recently published new edition of the 1 inch to 1 mile (1/63360) Ordnance Survey map of the area – Huddersfield, Sheet 102. I reckon this to be one of the best bargains I've ever had. At a cost of 3 shillings (15p in new money), which Mum generously paid, I became the proud possessor of a cloth edition, an item, although a bit grubby now, is still in my possession today. Armed with this on my rides, I could explore the district at will and I became something of an expert on the area. With a tiny compass in the top of a fountain pen, never once did I have a problem finding my way around and soon I was pretty accomplished at map reading too. I've never lost the love of maps and my subsequent career as a university senior lecturer in surveying, I'm sure, dates back to this early fascination with representing features on the earth's surface on a 'flat' piece of paper.

The physical difficulty of that one ride to Tinker's Monument also set me thinking about how it might be possible to modify my bike to ease the exertion. In the absence of an engine (incidentally clip-on petrol engines for bicycles were just becoming popular, but I was much too young to obtain a licence), I figured that what was needed were more gears and also a closer ratio between each. I'd spotted a derailleur gear manufactured by the Cyclo Company in Clarence Bradbury's bike shop window in Skelmanthorpe. This device, for some unexplained reason, seemed to be the preferred option on tandems. Different sized sprockets, usually 3, on the rear wheel were employed to alter the gear ratio. I thought it might be possible to combine the Sturmey Archer 3 speed hub gear with a 3 sprocket Cyclo derailleur mechanism, giving 9 gears in total. I convinced Dad this would work - as an engineer he could see the theory straight away.

Mum, in wanting to make my pedalling life easier, financed the project. What I had not foreseen, however, was that my bike chain stays were not wide enough to take 3 sprockets and moreover the rear wheel was not dished to accommodate them either. This did present a severe mechanical limitation and in the end I had to settle for only 2 sprockets, giving a total of 6 gears. I later realised that, by pure chance, one of the 2 new sprockets was larger than the original and the other one smaller. This gave me a higher top gear and a lower bottom gear and advantageously split the original 3 ratios to give 6 close ratio gears – altogether a pretty satisfactory outcome. This bike gave amazing service and I retained it as a 'hack' after a brand new one came along. My interest in and knowledge of cycling increased through my avid reading of *Cycling* magazine, which, in particular, introduced me to the racing scene. I became keen to participate, but the old Dawes was hardly up the task.

For a while I had been mildly pestering Mum about a racing bike when suddenly, out of the blue, she asked me if I had any particular model in mind. Too true I had. Reg Harris, world champion, rode one, the Raleigh Record Ace. I'd seen an example of this beautiful bronze coloured machine gleaming in the bike shop window in Wakefield. Its frame was Reynolds 531 double butted tubing, complemented by 27inch alloy wheel rims, large flange GB hubs, tubular tyres and fitted up with all the latest alloy components. As an out and out racing machine, it was a true thoroughbred. However, a price tag of £46-10s-6d (£46.53) was simply too much money for Mum and Dad. Nevertheless, I was surprised and more than delighted when they offered to buy me a brand new Raleigh Clubman – on the strict understanding that I would look after it and that this hobby wouldn't interfere with my school work and musical activities.

How could I refuse the second string of the Raleigh range? This bike had a blue Reynolds 531 frame with chrome fork ends and wheels with 27 inch stainless rims built on GB large flange hubs. The tyres were $1^1/_4$ inch section high pressures, which in truth were probably a better bet for a novice than the all out racing tubulars. Everything else was alloy including the casing of the medium ratio Sturmey Archer 3 speed hub gear. Mum and Dad also bought me a spare rear wheel for racing, which was a single fixed gear of, I think, about 80 inches. All this for £27-10s-0d (£27.50)! On reflection the package was ideal for both racing and touring. Stripped down for racing action the bike, I remember, weighed around 24lbs.

It was sheer luck that the nearest cycling club, Holme Valley Wheelers, ran a 10 mile time trial each Wednesday evening in the summer months on a course which passed right through Scissett. The start was along Kaye Line at Denby Dale on the A635 Barnsley to Holmfirth road. After about one mile, the route then joined the A636 through Scissett and the five-mile turn was some distance up Bentley Springs, the hill leading to Bretton Bar. The return leg followed exactly the same route in reverse. The trick in riding this course was to conserve just enough energy on the 'easy' outward leg, which was all down hill, to maintain a decent speed on the steady, but nagging, climb back to the start. The return leg contained one really punishing section through Denby Dale from the Salvation Army Citadel to the railway viaduct. It was probably only about a half mile in length, but it was relatively steep. By the time I was riding this part, the lungs were near bursting point and the legs were hurting badly. It was only the thought that I had completed nine tenths of the course that prevented me from climbing off the bike.

I rode this course many, many times in all weathers, but I absolutely hated rain. In truth, I was a bit of a wimp and it was an absolute certainty that DNS (Did Not Start) would appear against my name on the results board at the slightest drop of rain. My weather forecasting skill, however, was somewhat shaky and a sharp downpour occasionally caught me out. My best results on that course, which was not conducive to fast times, were around the 29 minute mark. I also rode several other courses in the flatter lands around Wakefield and, these being easier, I managed to reduce my best times to under 27 minutes.

Much as I enjoyed time trialing and the friendly competitive spirit of all participants, bicycle touring offered the even greater rewards of camaraderie and the pleasure of discovering new places, often in remote areas. Touring for me split into two distinct types. Day outings were the simplest to organise, whilst the longer tours of several days duration required rather more thought with regard to route and, naturally, overnight accommodation.

I never toured with the Holme Valley Wheelers but with mates from Scissett. The group was a fluid one and included John Booth, Gerald Fisher, Philip Tatchell and Gordon Robinson. The day's outings to the east and northeast were usually either to York and the surrounding flat lands, or to the Harrogate and Knaresborough districts. Although these were considered easy runs, there was always a sting in the tail. Heading back to Scissett out of Wakefield was the deceptively difficult climb up Bullcliffe. It didn't look much of a gradient, but there was no respite and it was well over a mile of unremitting toil, coming as it did at the end of a long day in the saddle. Any slight wind, which blew predominately from the west also tormented us on our homeward journeys. From Scissett it was roughly 40 miles to York and so, with detours, a run of something around 100 miles in the day was not uncommon. We usually carried our sandwiches for lunch and sampling one of the several fish and chip shops along the route always marked our return. A particular favourite of mine was in the village of Woodlesford, some 10 miles to the east of Wakefield – there was also another decent one in Stanley, more or less on the outskirts of Wakefield.

Our other main area for day exploration was to the south and west. Here the Pennine hills were far more vicious and a favourite route was through Penistone and Langsett then continuing over The Strines into Derbyshire. This minor road over the moors had not one, but three absolute 'leg breakers' all within a distance of about 7 miles. The first, traversing the Ewden Valley, was the real killer with gradients of 1 in 4. The remaining two valley crossings at Strines and Agden Bridge both exceeded 1 in 7. Favourite lunch stops were either at Ladybower Reservoir, Hathersage or Castleton. The return routes were certainly not easy ones and required more than a smidgen of strength, endurance and fitness to overcome the long climbs. The first stage was either via the Snake Pass (A57) or via the A525 and A624 through Chapel-en-le-Frith and Hayfield, both routes leading to Glossop on the Cheshire border. The climbs didn't end there, despite the fact that many times I wished they had done. A few miles after leaving Glossop and heading back into Yorkshire the choice was not a pleasant one. It was either the very difficult, steep and long climb over Holme Moss or the much longer drag but slightly kinder gradient up over the Woodhead Pass. These one-day rides had the advantage that if the weather was bad and didn't look like improving during the time we'd be on the road, then we simply didn't bother to start. I can't remember being caught out in rain or snow more than a couple of times.

Tours lasting several days were, of course, quite a different proposition. We were all members of the Youth Hostels Association (YHA) and used these excellent, but sometimes primitive, establishments for overnight accommodation. Having planned the route and booked our overnight stops, we were committed (I believe a condition of booking was to send a Postal Order for the cost in advance). I must say that most times we were lucky with the weather, but two occasions still live vividly in the memory. The first was on an Easter Monday, possibly in 1950, when we were caught out on the North Yorkshire Moors between Scarborough and Whitby in a tremendous snow blizzard. This unexpected challenge lasted virtually all day and I can still feel the biting north wind blasting the snow into my face and onto my bare legs. That day really was hard physically, since we were riding across open moorland for long stretches head-on into the driving snow. The only advantage of the sub-zero temperature was that the resulting snowflakes were light and fluffy and not the horrible heavy wet stuff.

The second occasion was on the ride home from a stay of several days in Bridlington, where incidentally we had blue skies and searing temperatures, which would not have disgraced the Mediterranean resorts. We spent lazy days down by the harbour fishing with hired rods with not a care in the world – despite best Yorkshire bait our determined efforts yielded nothing more than the occasional emaciated crab. When we awoke on our day of departure the sky was jet black and shortly after leaving the heavens opened. We huddled together in a bus shelter in a small village waiting for the torrential rain to pass. After some while we realised that this was not going to happen and we braced ourselves for the inevitable extreme unpleasantness, which we knew was our lot for the day. Seeing the sign announcing the name of a village we were about to enter on the A166 between Driffield and York lifted our spirits, at least temporarily. The name? *Wetwang.* I've often wondered how on earth the village managed to acquire such a strange name.

In contrast to our tours to the Yorkshire coast resorts of Bridlington, Scarborough, Filey, Whitby and other smaller fishing villages, our other main area of biking holidays took in the Yorkshire Dales. Our usual route northwards passed through an area renowned in the Brass Band world. First came the small town of Brighouse, base of undoubtedly the world's finest public subscription band, Brighouse and Rastrick. A few miles further on came the large village of Queensbury, home of arguably the world's most famous and successful band, Black Dyke Mills. From there our route passed through Bronte land, just skirting Haworth and a few miles further on at Keighley we left the industrial West Riding. The market towns of Skipton, Settle and Ingleton led to a variety of options for tours through the Yorkshire Dales. Magnificent scenery along every route and place names to conjure with – Kettlewell, Starbottom, Hubberholme, Muker, Arkengarthdale and Crackpot to name but a small sample. Our furthest point north that we ever reached was Bowes, over Tan Hill, the latter, reputedly being the location of the highest pub in the country. These rides into north Yorkshire had some pretty fearsome climbs, but we didn't seem to mind, knowing that a magnificent view awaited us and, of course, we'd the expectation of an exhilarating descent. Cyclists, in the main, don't object to climbing hills for there is always the payback of a good free wheel back down. No, the absolute hate is pedalling into a head wind all day – energy sapping and soul destroying it is, although some might class it as character building.

I was lucky to enjoy my youthful days cycling on quiet roads with very little danger from other traffic. On the road, the few cars were still the preserve of the 'well-off' and the odd goods vehicle was purely of the local delivery type since the railways still carried the majority of freight. I then had a break of several years from 'serious' cycling, but returned to it again in my late 30's when I spent a small fortune building a superb road bike with an Italian Alan frame, which I rode for thousands of miles, many abroad. Sadly, I gave up cycling again in my early 60's, not through lack of enthusiasm or energy, but simply because I felt the volume and speed of traffic made it far too dangerous. The car is now king. Sad isn't it?

8
FIRES, FAGS AND FIREWORKS

Bored? Never! Despite there being no television, no Gameboys, no computer games, no iPods, no MP3 players and not many toys, as boys growing up in the Upper Dearne Valley we had plenty to occupy our spare time in addition to participating in organised sporting and cultural activities. There could be no better playground than an area of intense industry surrounded by fields and woods. I must confess that several of our activities were on the fringes of the law and if we'd done such things today we'd certainly be on the receiving end of ASBOs (Anti Social Behaviour Orders). That said, we never committed mindless vandalism or property damage, neither did we deliberately go out to steal (other than apples) nor to harm people. The Remand Home for young offenders at Nortonthorpe Hall on the outskirts of the village was a continual reminder of the severe punishment that such behaviour could bring. Although it was something of a rough and ready area, we had great respect for our parents and our elders.

Fires seemed to hold a strange fascination for growing lads and if we had built a camp in the woods or in a haystack it was incomplete without a campfire. Our parents forbade us from having fires, but this was no real deterrent. If we had transgressed, my mother could usually smell the wood smoke on my clothes and then I'd be in for a severe 'telling off'. We always attempted to control any fires we lit, but on several occasions these either got out of control or sparks from them ignited nearby vegetation. This led to several near disasters and one utter calamity. Several of our campfires in the Duke Wood went out of control and I remember tearing down tree branches and beating the flames furiously to prevent them spreading.

The one occasion when things went disastrously wrong was a campfire in a haystack in one of farmer Horace Brook's fields.

Try as we might, we could not control its spread. Realising the hopelessness of our task and scared out of our wits, we fled the scene. The fire was soon spotted and Horace and his farm hands soon had it under control. We guessed that Horace would soon pay a visit to Scissett Junior School in search of the culprits. In our scramble to leave the now established blaze one of us left his cap, which had his initials inside. It didn't take a genius to work out the owner of this incriminating evidence. Back in school he was put under considerable pressure to reveal the identities of his confederates. Eventually the names spilled out and we all received a severe caning.

The huge bonfires we built to celebrate Guy Fawkes night were indeed spectacular. The fires were situated right on the edge of the steep Pit Hill overlooking the village. To spectators in the village some 150 feet below, the sight of the fiercely blazing fire must have been awesome. For several weeks in advance we had chopped down, quite illegally, substantial fir trees from the plantation in Wheatley Hill and dragged these by rope to the chosen spot. Sufficient time elapsed to allow them to dry out so that small kindling and a good dousing with paraffin would fairly readily ignite them. These trunks contained substantial quantities of resin, which caused them to burn with great intensity.

The Wheatley Hill plantation was rather small, but the district had some pretty big woods, including Duke Wood, Kitchenroyd Wood, Cuttlehurst Wood, Hay Royds Wood and the monster Deffer Wood. It was not surprising that most youngsters from the district were expert tree climbers and those who indulged in the 'sport' thoroughly enjoyed the thrill of climbing some of the very tall specimens. Our competitive natures often came to the fore and we'd vie with each other to climb to the highest position up a particular tree. The undoubted star was Melvin Lodge, a true daredevil, who seemed to defy gravity. He could shin up large girth beech trees, which often had few branches to aid the ascent. I can't ever remember anyone suffering a serious injury, although one or two minor falls did happen. Looking back, that really was a miracle considering we were often about 45metres above the ground clinging on for dear life to a swaying trunk, which had slimmed down to a few centimetres and what's more the branches supporting our feet weren't much thicker than matchsticks. A favourite pastime, also involving trees, was to carve our names on them, with beech, because of its reasonably smooth bark, being the favoured medium. I know that several of my efforts, even after some 60 years have elapsed, are still extant.

Fireworks played an important role in our lives too. During the war, sales of these were banned. Just after the war I remember hearing that the Marsden's shop in Clayton West had some pre-war stock on sale and friend Garth and myself managed to purchase a dozen bangers. These were 'Little Demons' manufactured by Lion Fireworks. I believe they cost only a half penny each in old money, equivalent to 0.21p!! Despite their cheapness, they went off with a hell of a bang. In view of the age of the stock, it's hardly surprising that out of the dozen we bought, about 5 were duds and didn't explode – the fuse just fizzed. Determined to get our money's worth, we lit a small fire in the disused quarry behind Teddy Blackburn's mill air-raid shelter. We let the fire burn for a while to get some hot glowing ashes and then buried the bundle of duds in the ashes. We retired to a safe distance and waited a while, but to our deep disappointment, absolutely nothing happened!! We approached gingerly and eventually plucked up courage to poke the ashes with sticks. We were bending down about a couple of feet away when the lot exploded. It was a miracle that the explosion didn't burst our eardrums and the cloud of hot ashes didn't blind us for life. However, and I'm not exaggerating, the ringing noises in our ears lasted for days.

Huddersfield is an amazing town for all sorts of reasons, but I'm at a complete loss to explain why the majority of the country's fireworks output was produced there. Lion Fireworks had a very large complex at Lepton, about 3 miles to the east of the town centre, whilst the rival Standard Fireworks factory was on the opposite side of town, at Crosland Moor, no more than a couple of miles from the town centre. We used to have long discussions trying to decide who made the best ones – some youngsters supported Lion others Standard, much like football fans support their favourite teams. I don't think that the argument was ever settled conclusively, but my choice was Lion.

Despite the ready availability of fireworks after the war I decided, when I was about 12 years old, it would be a good idea to manufacture a more powerful banger. My first choice of explosive was gunpowder, for the ingredients were easily obtainable. Saltpetre could be bought over the counter in Clifford Thompson's chemist shop in the village, sulphur was a chemical in every schoolboy's chemistry set and charcoal could be manufactured by incinerating wood shavings. My chemistry laboratory was Mum's disused wash-kitchen round the back of the house. For the banger casing I used compressed cardboard bobbins from Teddy Blackburn's mill. I tried various proportions of the constituents and rammed them hard into the bobbin. Although I managed to get some pretty impressive flashes, indicating rapid combustion, the holy grail of the experiments, a loud explosion, eluded my determined efforts. It was only years later, when studying explosives as part of a mining engineering degree, that I realised that my problem lay in the grain size. I simply had been unable to grind the mixture down into small enough particles to give a large enough total surface area, which was essential for instantaneous combustion.

Undeterred, I changed tack entirely and decided that the future of my pyrotechnic research lay in an explosive called Gun Cotton. I had a thick encyclopaedia with a whole chapter devoted to industrial chemistry. One section dealt with explosives including Gun Cotton and TNT. The manufacture of the latter sounded complicated so I opted for a seemingly straightforward process to produce Gun Cotton. The 2 ingredients were cotton, which was in plentiful supply in the form of thread from Teddy Blackburn's mill and concentrated nitric acid. Today, it seems almost inconceivable that as a youngster I could get my hands on as much of this dangerous substance as I wanted, but remember this was at a time when the advent of the Health & Safety Executive

(HSE) was some 40 years in the future. Glass carboys each containing around 30 gallons of concentrated acids, hydrochloric, sulphuric and nitric used in cloth dying were kept out in the open, without any form of security, at the side of Wood Street mill. Simple for me to take out the large glass stopper, lower a glass bottle on a length of wire into the liquid and hey presto - a seemingly unlimited supply of concentrated nitric acid. Because there was so much available for the taking, it never entered my head that I was stealing. The encyclopaedia description of the manufacture of Gun Cotton was deceptively simple: *The high explosive is produced by treating cotton with concentrated nitric acid.* I followed this instruction, but still that magic explosion eluded me. Why? I've no idea. I then considered the manufacture of TNT, but this sounded beyond my capability. Undoubtedly, my failure to produce gunpowder and Gun Cotton and the complexity of TNT's manufacture probably saved me from serious injury at the least, if not an early demise. Luck again eh?

I've had few pieces of bad luck in life, but one did occur in that very same quarry where Garth and I had nearly blown our heads off with the bundle of fireworks. The stroke of sheer bad luck cut short my initiation into smoking. As boys, tobacco was strictly off limits for us, despite the fact that most adult males seemed to puff away like chimneys either with cigarettes or with a pipe. It was only natural that we should want to sample, what seemed to us, a forbidden delight. The problem, of course, was getting hold of contraband smoking materials. I was about 10 years old, and quite unexpectedly one day, my friend, Garth (yes him again!), called on me. He'd been brave enough to pinch two Players Navy Cut cigarettes and a few matches from his father. Off we went to the old quarry and there deemed it safe enough to light up. I suppose we'd been enjoying the experience for about three minutes, when a booming voice rang out, *"Hellewell, get yourself up here now!"* What appalling luck! It was my Dad, who just happened, at that time, to be walking up the road alongside the quarry wall and spotted the rising cigarette smoke. He peeped over into the quarry below and saw both of us puffing away like mad. Garth, quite rightly, shot off like a scalded cat and left me to face the music. Such a serious offence merited a real good hiding, which Dad duly administered.

The hard frosts and snows of winter were invariably greeted with jubilation by the youngsters. I believe it is a fact that the winters of the 1940's were much more severe than now. Indeed, it would have been exceptional if several good snowfalls, with snow lying for at least several days, had not occurred each year. Sledges, mostly home made affairs, were brought out of storage, their iron runners polished up with emery cloth, and off we went to the steep slopes along Scissett Common. The two favourite runs were in the Paraffin Field on the south side of the Common and the 'Big Dipper' on the north side. The Paraffin Field was a thrilling, challenging run because of the severe bumps remaining from strip farming and the limited stopping distance to the stone boundary wall. By contrast the Big Dipper was a smoother run, but the gradient was severe – I guess somewhere in the region of 1 in 3. The descents achieved on a hard packed icy track were like greased lightening and ensured a huge adrenalin rush. At the bottom of the run, it was essential to deliberately throw ones self off the sledge to avoid heading through the ice into the freezing water of Marshall Mill dam.

After sledging for an afternoon our clothes were often quite wet and the cold gradually began to bite. Of course, boys didn't wear long trousers until they were about 13 years old and our knees became chapped and extremely painful for long periods during the winter – the palliative treatment was a daily application of *Snowfire,* obtainable in those days from the local Co-op.

Some periods during the winter months were free of snow, but were often well below freezing throughout the day. The several sizeable dams in the district froze over with ice thick enough to skate on. I had inherited a pair of skates from uncle Colin and I taught myself to skate reasonably proficiently. The large man-made upper lake in Bretton Park, a short bike ride away, was a beautiful, peaceful spot and I enjoyed many happy hours there.

The lake was about half a mile long and with a following breeze the speeds that could be achieved were exhilarating. Of course, one paid for that with the return skate being a real sweat into the headwind. On several occasions, members of the Earnshaw family, who owned the wood yard at Midgely turned up with their friends and a car full of hockey sticks and I was always invited to join in their game.

Incidentally, in the early 1960's, I had the good fortune to purchase a double bass from the same family. This bass, named many years later by Norman Mason, a former Halle and BBC Welsh Symphony Orchestra professional, *The Little Gem*, has been a lifelong companion.

The winter of 1947 will always remain in my memory, for it was one of the most exciting and happiest few months of my boyhood. It was, according to official records the most severe winter of the 20th century. Following a comparatively mild start to the year, the bitter east wind arrived on the 20th January and with it a heavy snowfall, which paralysed the transport system for several days. I remember waking up in the morning, looking through the bedroom window and seeing the top of a one metre high wall opposite the house just poking through the snow, such was the severity of the overnight blizzard. Little did I realise at the time just how desperate life would become. The country was paralysed, exacerbated by an acute fuel shortage, which had a knock on effect for industry still on its knees only 2 years after the war's end and once again many foods were in short supply.

For several days the feeble snow plough, which was no more than an angled blade attached to the front of the council lorry, attempted to clear the main roads. After a considerable struggle the major routes of the district were reopened, some only being wide enough for a single vehicle with the occasional passing place. The situation really was desperate and German prisoners of war from nearby camps were drafted in to help with the

Mum and myself standing in the snow on Cuttlehurst Hill
1947
Snow reaches the top of the metre high wall opposite my
home.

clearance. Many minor roads, including Cuttlehurst Hill, where I lived, Wheatley Hill and Scissett Common never received civic attention and local residents shovelled the snow away as best they could. Of course, we youngsters just loved this sort of activity. The snow had drifted deeply in many places and I remember walking on top of the frozen surface of 3metre high drifts in Wheatley Hill. The numerous small mixed farms, such as those at Toppit, which were off the main routes had a precarious time. Milk from these farms was eventually moved by horse drawn sledge.

For me, the remarkable feature of this winter was not simply its severity but its duration. Snow lay deep for the remainder of January, the whole of February and for much of March. There were long periods when the days were extremely cold and, despite the sun shining from a cloudless blue sky, hardly any snow melted and that which did formed a hard ice crust. Official figures record 34 days when the temperature failed to climb above freezing even at mid-day. However, the bright, crisp conditions were exhilarating provided one was reasonably well wrapped up with wool jumper, scarf, balaclava and gloves. These long stable periods were interspersed with the odd couple of days when the sky turned a thick grey hue and yet another heavy snowstorm was upon us. This weather pattern lasted well into March. Many times, the schools in the district were closed and those remaining open often had a large crop of absentees, although I can't ever recall missing a day.

The deep snow prevented our use of sledges in the fields so several of the youngsters, myself included, managed to fabricate crude skis. We had seen Noel Beardsall, a director of Beanland's mill travelling around on his proper ones and we were determined to emulate him. The trickiest problems were producing a reasonable upturn at the ski front end and also devising a reliable ski binding. After several trials, I finally produced a fairly good practical effort. The former problem I solved by using an elementary steam box to bend the wood, whilst my bindings utilised long coil springs from an old loom. I even managed to cut a shallow groove down the sole of each ski and before each use I applied a generous coating of candle wax. After some practice I became quite proficient and was able to execute turns and control downhill runs. I found skiing far more satisfying than sledging and also tremendous fun. Without making further modifications, I used these skis for several years.

The local mills also provided a playground for the youngsters daring enough to carry out a spot of trespass. Norton's Nortonthorpe Mill was one of our prime targets. It had been discovered that a window in the long shed, which had been built across the River Dearne, was insecure. This side of the building was well away from Cuttlehurst Hill and hidden from view by a small wood. A gentle push on the frame would open the window and a scramble up off the ground would see us head first through the window opening. A bit of a contortion would then allow us to drop feet first onto the interior floor. Once inside we struck gold. An electric trolley was housed in there and it didn't take us long to work out its modus operandi. Soon we were flying up and down the length of the shed and performing the trolley equivalent of hand brake turns. The trolley, being driven by an electric motor, was almost silent and so we could entertain ourselves at the weekend without fear of being discovered. I'm absolutely amazed that none of the mill employees twigged what was going on, for on several occasions the trolley ended up with a flat battery through our continual use. The only mishap I can recall was an incident when one of us succeeded in driving a wheel of the trolley over Charles Wilkinson's foot. That certainly made Charles jump around a bit and it's a wonder he hadn't any broken toes or foot bones.

The noisy and smelly interior of the mills never held any fears for me. I can remember many occasions when my grandfather, George Hellewell, who was manager of the Nortonthorpe Mill, walked me around the factory. I was his only grandchild and I think it was for him a source of considerable pleasure to show me off from a very young age to the factory workers. He always took me into the weaving shed where the cacophony of the countless

Double Dobcross looms assaulted my ears – it was almost impossible to communicate without shouting into the listener's ear and sign language amongst the girls at the looms had reached an advanced level. He delighted to take me to the quieter boiler house and open the firebox door of one of the Lancashire boilers to reveal a roaring inferno. His favourite treat was to show off the gleaming mill steam engine, *Violet*, and today I'm still able to recall the 'chuff- chuff' of this mighty beast. Of course, granddad had begun his career as a mechanic in the mill, rising eventually to chief engineer before becoming manager and naturally he was steeped in the world of steam.

Before I had even started going to school I was a daily visitor in Edward Blackburn's Cuttlehurst Mill. The mill was adjacent to where I lived and I'd only to toddle some 20metres or so through the small mill yard and in at the main door of the 3 storey building. In the mornings I used to lie awake in bed listening to the clatter and chatter of the mill girls walking up Cuttlehurst Hill in readiness for a 7.00am start. The noise from the working mill was an ever present in our house, so I was able to listen for the mill engine stopping signalling the daily 8.30am breakfast break. This was my cue to dash out of the house, through the mill's main door, turn first left and down to the far aisle where Lucy Shaw would meet me with outstretched arms. Lucy earned her living as a bobbin winder. She had to be physically strong to lug the full bobbin boxes around, yet she had a gentle nature. More than that, she was a lovely lady who picked me up like a little doll and sat me down on her bobbin box, my legs dangling off the ground. Invariably she sat alongside me and gave me a little of her breakfast. I was fascinated by the little stories she told me and she even explained and showed me the intricacies of her winding frame. I adored her and in later life I felt sad that she and her husband, Edward, had no children – I know she would have been a marvellous Mum. I met Lucy occasionally later in life and we always chatted about those very happy times.

Although I knew well the inside of Teddy Blackburn's mill, it was on the outside that we lads got up to our tricks. The small mill yard had large boxes and baskets stacked up, perhaps to a height of 5metres. We'd climb up onto the top of these and jump into the topmost open baskets. Often the stack of baskets would come crashing down and we'd be hurled out onto the yard's concrete floor sometimes ending up with scraped hands and knees. The manager of the mill at that time was Walter Hardcastle, who lived a hundred metres higher up Cuttlehurst Hill. We weren't particularly afraid of him but if he found us on the premises he'd shout at us and send us away, threatening to tell our parents, which curiously, he never did. Another game we used to play involved stretching many lengths of cotton thread across the road and then hiding under the lean-to open shed immediately at the side of the road to view proceedings. Of course, we were amused when pedestrians got themselves caught up in the cotton and it was difficult to suppress our laughter at the antics of some who were trying to extricate themselves from the tangle. On one occasion we were seriously worried. A flashy sports car driven at speed by Margaret Kaye's husband suddenly screeched to a halt. He leapt out in a flash and shouting angrily, rushed over to the shed. It seemed as though he might discover our hiding place, drag us out and give us a good hiding. We all held our breath and I could feel my heart pounding, but he drove off and the danger passed.

When I was about 11 years old, for once I found myself at a loose end one Saturday afternoon. For want of anything better to do, I climbed over the wall at the bottom of Cuttlehurst and discovered the entrance to a tunnel disappearing under the road. The entrance was inside a small brick enclosure, open at the front, and perhaps 4metres above the river. The tunnel itself was a circular cross section about one metre diameter and lined with, what appeared to be, sections of iron Lancashire boiler fire tubes. Peering in, once my eyes were accustomed to the poor light, I could just make out a faint light at the other end. The temptation was simply too great! I decided there and then, without the benefit of a torch, to explore this new mystery. I crawled though comfortably on hands and knees and eventually emerged in a small room in Hirst Buckley's printing works at the other side of the road. This housed a small steam driven pump and I realised then that the steam supply pipe from the Nortonthorpe Mill boiler house on the other side of the road passed through the tunnel. It struck me then that the tunnel was rather over-engineered simply to carry a steam pipe of a measly 5cm diameter.

Several times over the next few months I returned to examine the machinery and gradually I figured out how to operate it. Eventually I plucked up courage and soon had the little reciprocating steam engine running quite sweetly. Then, to my horror it began to struggle and slow down almost to a stop. Quick as a flash I closed the steam inlet valve. Stupidly, I had failed to open the delivery valve on the pump's rising main. Afterwards, I learned that because the pump was of the positive displacement type, tremendous pressure could build up on the delivery side if the outlet valve remained closed. Perhaps a few more seconds and the pump would have burst causing me serious injury. How's that for luck again? Although I was unaware at the time of a potential pump explosion, curiously the incident frightened me and I dared not tell anyone.

There were 3 other tunnels, which discharged water into the river. The mouths were stone lined arches and each headed off under Hirst Buckley's printing works. In times of heavy rain, water gushed out into the river and during dry spells the tunnel floors appeared to be covered in thick mud deposits. Although I was tempted to explore them to discover where they led, their sinister character always deterred me and I also reckoned they would be the home to several rat families – enough to put off any youngster. Whilst I cannot be sure, I presume they came out to day light somewhere near the 3 dams in Bagden Lane.

The 3 dams in Bagden Lane, which had served the now defunct Norton's Cuttlehurst Mill, were disused, but the lower one was still in good condition and about 1.5 metres deep. Several times we made large rafts and spent our afternoons sailing around. We had plenty of old wood from the ruined mill to construct the raft's platform and for buoyancy we employed empty oil drums lashed underneath. I remember one effort in particular, when we acquired a beautiful arched wooden window frame, some 3 metres from the top of the arch to the base and we nailed to this a platform of old mill floorboards. Looking back, I now realise how dangerous our maritime efforts might appear, although I cannot remember anyone going overboard. In any event, most of us were good swimmers and the real danger lay in getting tangled with reeds on the bottom. It was uppermost in our minds that a 16 year old lad had drowned recently when swimming in the Square Wood Resevoir at Denby Dale.

I truly count myself lucky to have been born and brought up in the Upper Dearne Valley and Scissett in particular. For growing lads it was just like a modern adventure park, but with one important difference. It was free! I was fortunate too to be one of a group of youngsters who grew up together and had plenty of spirit and determination to explore and enjoy what this rough and ready district had to offer. Amongst my many friends from those days Garth Hutchinson, John Hallas, Gordon Beaumont (sadly died in 2006), Richard Haigh, Charles Wilkinson, Gerald Fisher, Melvin Lodge, John Booth, Gordon Robinson, Phillip Tatchell and David Exley   shared many of those escapades. They were a lively lot and, believe me, in their company there was never a dull moment.

10

STRINGS AND BRASS

It is always said that to be successful in music one should begin early. Well I'm not so sure about success in my case, but begin early I certainly did. My career in symphony orchestras and other ensembles began at the age of 9. I recall that my first symphony concert was sitting at the back of the second violins in a small orchestra conducted by Milton Beever. I had great respect for Milton, since he was a kind sympathetic man and he, unlike several other conductors I've met in my long musical career, never showed up a player who simply 'could not get it right'. He was a secondary school teacher in Barnsley, a cellist and keen amateur musician, who had assembled this small orchestra in his home village of Denby Dale. Most members, if not all, were adults and I was by far the youngest. The orchestra was led by my violin teacher, Willie Kaye, so an invitation to join this group at such an early age is unsurprising since it originated with him. The concerts were held in the Memorial Hall at Denby Dale attached to the Centenary Methodist Chapel in Cumberworth Road. I don't remember much about my first concert except that the programme included Hayden's Surprise Symphony and that my chair had a terrible squeak.

For my seventh birthday, my parents had bought me a violin from a chap called Charlie Lockwood who lived in Emley. I remember that they paid £5 for it. I suppose that was a fair price, given that the average week's wage was considerably less. I still own this instrument today, mainly for sentimental reasons. Some years later, I found out that the violin, made around 1870, is a German Markneukirchen copy of a double purfled Italian Maggini.

The question of lessons then became a major discussion and in the end I was sent to Willie Kaye, who I believe was an Emley man, but at the time was living in Penistone Road, Kirkburton.

Willie was a young-looking, tall, debonair man with slicked down black hair, typical of the time. I liked Willie, for he always taught by example and was quick to praise a good effort. On the other hand, he could be quite a 'stickler' for accuracy and quick to reproach if I'd shirked practice during the last week – he claimed he could always tell immediately if I'd missed out on daily practice. Willie had been a pupil of Laurence Turner, originally from Huddersfield, who served many years as leader of the Halle. Willie was a good technician on the fiddle and, I believe, as a young man before the war also had a spell with the Halle. When I went for lessons during the war, he was working as an overlooker at Springrove Mills, Kirkburton and I assume this must have been a reserved occupation, unless he was too old to have been called up into the services, his youthful looks disguising his true age. Willie was the local 'fixer' who organised and led all the ad-hoc orchestras for the multitude of amateur operatic societies, choirs etc which performed regularly in the villages of the district.

My first lesson with Willie was on 21st March 1943. I can even remember Willie telling me at the start of the lesson that I would always remember that date since it was the first day of spring. The 10 mile round trip to Kirkburton was made by bus, at first accompanied by Mum, but then as I became accustomed to the journey I tackled it alone from that summer onward. The lessons were one and a half hours long and at the end of it I'd hand over a silver 2 shilling (20p) piece – quite a bargain. After I'd done my bit in the lesson, Willie always played the exercises and pieces he'd set me, just to reinforce what I was aiming at. During the last few minutes he always played for me something more advanced, such as excerpts from concertos, sonatas or some 'showy' piece of Kreisler or Paganini. I just loved these impromptu performances and I looked forward to the day when, hopefully, I'd be able to emulate him.

In the main, I did practice diligently and I had soon reached the end of my fairly thick tutor book. After completing this, Willie then introduced several books full of nothing but graded exercises, including the famous studies by Kayser and Sevcik, the latter dealing entirely with bowing. These exercises were simply to develop a decent technique. In addition, we worked on solos, including easier bits of concertos, in order to encourage musicality – phrasing, rubato, interpretation and such like.

Whilst still in junior school I played many times in concerts both in Scissett and surrounding villages. These were variety concerts, purely for entertainment and consequently none too highbrow. For example, my contribution could be wedged between a dialect recitation of *Albert and the Lion* and a vocalist giving a rendition of *The Lost Chord*. In that context, 'serious' fiddle pieces were out of the question and I relied on such favourites as *Staendchen*, made famous by Albert Sandler, and *Roses From The South*. Occasionally I'd slip in Bach's *Air on the G string* or Handel's *Largo*. To put it mildly, pianos in village, church and chapel halls were of variable quality, and Mum, who accompanied me, had often to contend with sticking keys and squeaky pedals. I certainly enjoyed playing these concerts and they never caused me any anxiety since the pieces had been well prepared and were well within my capability. If I made the odd small slip from time to time, the audience certainly didn't seem to notice.

After 4 years of playing and at the age of 11, I turned professional. Again, I've Willie's fixing ability to thank for that. He asked me if I'd be interested in joining his little 'pit' band playing for shows put on by local societies doing operettas, pantomimes etc. Too true I would! At a fee of between 10 shillings (50p) and 30 shillings (£1.50) for a band call, 4 weeknights, Saturday evening and the occasional Saturday matinee, the money was just too good to miss. But more than that – it was good fun too. I don't remember many of the personnel except Willie who led, Victor Senior, my second fiddle desk partner and Albion Burt on cello.

Brass and woodwind players were engaged on an occasional basis depending on the requirements of the orchestration. The pianists were always provided by the society, since these brave souls had slogged through weeks of rehearsals with the cast. Scissett

Amateur Operatic Society's pianist was a bubbly young lady, Winnie Firth, who used to chat to me and make me feel very much at home. She later became Winnie Adamski on marriage. The societies also provided the conductor, who again had taken all the rehearsals. The outstanding ones were Stephen Wray at Scissett and Mrs Pobjoy, at Emley. She was a brilliant musician, who also happened to be the Rector's wife. Mrs Pobjoy's talents extended to writing both the script and the music for many of the Emley shows, these, of course, being absolutely original productions. Of all the shows, for me, the most memorable was *'The Boyfriend'* at Scissett, in which the lead was taken by a pretty teenager, Barbara Gill, with whom I instantly fell in love.

'Sings' were another musical event in which I participated. These were open-air vocal gatherings, very popular in the Barnsley and Huddersfield areas, (they may even have been limited to these districts) and they were held during the afternoon of the Feast Sunday of a particular village. An ad-hoc choir, raised from the local churches and chapels, often numbering a hundred or more voices, sang well-loved hymns and oratorio choruses, with the spectators joining in. The singers were elevated on a temporary tiered wooden staging with the orchestra arrayed in front at ground level. Since there was no control on the standard of players who turned up on a particular day, or indeed the numbers and instrumentation, at times some peculiar sounds emanated from these ad-hoc ensembles. Almost invariably, the choruses were *Hallelujah*, *And the Glory* and *Worthy is the Lamb* from Handel's Messiah, but occasionally the *Gloria* from Mozart's 12th Mass and Hayden's *The Heavens are Telling* received an airing. During these afternoon proceedings the local brass band would play a couple of selections too. Three of the best Sings, in my book, were Kirkburton held on Trinity Sunday, Skelmanthorpe in early July and Longwood, in the Colne Valley, in early September.

The competitive side of violin playing was an aspect I never enjoyed, although to please Mum, Dad and Willie I did submit to the ordeal. There were several large musical festivals with age group classes for violin. From about the age of 10, I took part in competitions in Leeds, Bradford, Keighley, Holmfirth and also the *Mrs Sunderland* at Huddersfield, which was looked on as the 'home' event. For competition work, it was thought I ought to have a better sounding violin. In recent years I've found out that the violin I then acquired was old English or possibly Scottish; it has been variously dated between 1780 and 1840. I still have it today. I never won any of the competitions I entered, but I usually came in the top 10 of 30 plus entrants - I even made it into the top 3 on occasion. The large amount of preparation and practice I put into the various test pieces seemed out of all proportion to the enjoyment I derived from actually playing the pieces, many of which weren't all that tuneful. Performing in front of an eagle-eyed adjudicator and a super-critical audience was nerve racking, to say the least.

A notable fellow competitor was Rodney Friend from Bradford, who eventually became leader of both the BBC Symphony Orchestra and the London Symphony Orchestra. Rodney always performed without music and I remember thinking at the time what a marvellous memory he must have. It was only later I realised that this feat was probably due to the sheer volume of practice he'd done on each piece. Needless to say, I can't recall Rodney ever being beaten.

Although I'd been losing interest in violin playing for some time (I just didn't seem to have the enthusiasm to practice any longer), my violin playing career was ended suddenly by one competition. I was about 14 at the time and it was the *Mrs Sunderland* held in St Paul's Schoolroom, Huddersfield. The piece was a difficult one (can't remember the title) and cruelly it started with a harmonic D, which, under the stress of competition many of the performers failed to produce. I thought I had given a tidy performance, and whilst waiting for the results several in the audience complimented me. The adjudicator, however, had different ideas. His written remarks concentrated entirely on what he considered to be a faulty technique – no mention whatsoever of my actual performance and what I sounded like. He placed me

30 something. I was so disheartened I resolved there and then to finish playing completely. Mum, Dad and Willie were terribly upset and disappointed at my decision, but they accepted it with good grace. Looking back, I realise that my technique could have been better by accepted standards and was almost certainly the result of playing on a full size violin from the outset when I was too small to handle it properly. My bow tended to arc and my left wrist occasionally dropped to the neck to support the weight. However, to this day I still believe it is the result that matters not the way of achieving it.

Truth to tell, I missed violin playing not a jot. Some months elapsed and I just happened to call round to see a friend, John Hallas, whose father, George, was the conductor of Clayton West Brass Band. John, incidentally, was already playing in the band on third cornet. I knew George from his occasional appearances playing trumpet in Willie's Kaye's 'pit' band. He'd heard that I'd stopped fiddling and offered me the opportunity to try an old trombone, which had been lying around in the band room for years. I was keen to give it a go and it was arranged for Albert Wood, a trombone player in the band, to teach me. That old Boosey trombone really was past it, for I remember Albert having to solder the inner slide to the cross stay before it was usable. Needless to say the slide action was dreadful and no amount of different lubrication concoctions would improve it.

I had several months of free private lessons from Albert, mastering the blowing and slide positions in both the treble and tenor clefs. I could read music so that didn't present any problems and it was therefore mainly a matter of building up a decent embouchure and lip stamina, which only time and practice can do. Before too long, a reshuffle took place in the band and the 2nd trombone chair became vacant. Solo trombonist Albert thought I was capable of filling it and so I joined him and bass trombonist, Phillip Hallas, (George's brother) as a full band member. I was delighted that a much better Boosey trombone went with the position.

Joining that particular band was an amazing piece of luck. The bandsmen taught me such a lot, not just about music, but about life too. I had now moved into an adult world and my whole boyish attitude to life changed. I wanted to succeed as a trombone player and was prepared to work very hard to achieve that goal. I now became part of a wonderful diverse group of players who took me under their wing. The players were all working class, grafting hard in manual jobs. The 'corner men' of the band had a variety of jobs. Solo cornet Arthur Exley and solo euphonium Ned Mosley were foundrymen at Addy's Foundry in Clayton West, solo horn Alf Haigh worked underground at Park Mill colliery, soprano cornet Dennis Tucker was an overlooker at Beanland's mill and solo trombone Albert Wood was a painter and decorator. Educationally, they had never had much of a chance in life, yet they were intelligent people with wide ranges of interest. Despite their lack of formal academic qualifications they, nevertheless, encouraged me to take up technical studies when I started work.

As a grammar school boy I'd led something of a sheltered life, never having come into really close contact with working men. In truth, I was taken aback by their talents and willingness to pass on their hard-earned knowledge and experience to me. First and foremost, they were keen, skilled musicians and for me a great inspiration. The band's conductor, George Hallas, was an excellent cornet player, who had played with Brighouse & Rastrick Band and, I believe, the CWS Band in Manchester. George was quietly spoken in rehearsal, but nevertheless authoritative, and he knew precisely the musical interpretation he wanted. I'm indeed grateful for the training and advice I received from him. My best mate in the band was bass trombone colleague, Phillip Hallas. Phillip had served in the Kings Own Yorkshire Light Infantry (KOYLI) in the 2nd War and had endured incredible hardship and horrors fighting the Japanese in the jungles of Burma in both campaigns. Although Phillip was some 17 years older than I, he certainly looked after me, almost like a son initially then, as time passed, we simply became best mates. On band engagements we were pretty much inseparable

Clayton West Band, 1952

Back row from left: D. Tucker, A. Exley, K. Wood, C. Horsley, F. Haigh, J. Speight, J. Hallas, D. Townsend, M. Firth, L. Haigh, B. Crossland

Middle row from left: P. Hallas, Myself, A. Thomas, A. Haigh, E. Cunningham, R. Wood, F. Mosley, J. Barker

Front row from left: W. Addy, L. Wainwright, E. Mosley, N. Beardsall (Band President), G. Hallas (Conductor), B. Smith, A. Wood, R. Cunningham

and on the long coach journeys we always sat next to each other and chatted the hours away.

Playing in the band opened up a whole new vista of musical experience and introduced me to some of the great classical compositions as well as many original brass band pieces. As well as the big name composers, I also came to know many of classical music's lesser-known ones such as Balfe, Wallace, Reisiger, Boildieu and Auber – names hardly known today and whose tuneful compositions are now rarely heard. I'd never played a march before, but soon found myself thrilled to be belting out the 'bass solos' of such favourites as *Slaidburn, BB&CF, Punchinello* and many others. From the orchestral repertoire I was excited by the arrangements of overtures with *Poet And Peasant, Morning, Noon and Night, The Caliph of Baghdad, Tancredi, Light Cavalry* and *The Mill on the Cliff* being particular favourites. At that time, the band world also relied on arrangements of the classics and of selections from operas and operettas. From my very early days in banding, I remember playing an arrangement of Dvorak's symphony *From the New World,* and selections from Wallace's *Maritana* and Balfe's *The Bohemian Girl.* Special to me was William Rimmer's fantasia on *Rule Britannia,* a stirring piece but with a contrasting quiet trombone trio, which was a great joy to play. I'm delighted that this work has been revived and recorded in recent years by the Fodens Courtois band. The engagements the band undertook were concerts in churches and chapels, open-air performances in the parks (Greenhead Huddersfield, Wilthorpe Barnsley, Normanton etc) and accompanying parades. The band hadn't entered brass band contests for many years probably the last one was pre-war.

Conductor George decided that the best way to improve our playing standard, although then by no means mediocre, was through the contest arena. It was in the early 1950's that bands were beginning to decline in popularity. Locally, both Denby and Denby Dale bands folded around this time through lack of players. We were fortunate to enlist some very good players from Denby Dale, which pre–war had an excellent record and had even done wireless broadcasts. Edwin Cunningham on tenor horn and his father Raymond on Bflat bass, Clifford Horsely on cornet and an excellent trombonist, Alan Thomas joined within a short time. The latter player released Albert Wood to move from solo trombone to Eflat bass. The band had always rehearsed twice a week on Tuesday and Friday evenings and now, because of our serious commitment to contesting, a third rehearsal was scheduled for Sunday afternoons.

Since the band had no recent track record we were automatically placed in the lowest (4th section) of the Daily Herald championship structure. Our first outing was to the North East Region contest at Huddersfield Town Hall, the test piece being an original band work, *Wayside Scenes,* by J.A. Greenwood. I don't remember much about the piece except it had a trombone trio about half way through. There were well over 30 bands entered and we were placed a creditable 4th. To be part of an event with so many bands competing (the 2nd section with some 20 bands also played in the evening) really made me proud to belong to this great movement. Our first win, playing an arrangement of Beethoven's *Mignon,* was several weeks later in May at the Belle Vue contest.

The band continued to perform well in contests and I have an outstanding memory of playing next year in the Daily Herald 3rd section at Leeds Town Hall. There I met a charming girl, Grace Dinsdale, who was principal cornet with the York Railway Institute Band. It was very rare in those days to have girls in bands, let alone one playing top cornet. Truth to tell, I was captivated by her. The evening contest for championship section bands including such illustrious names as Black Dyke Mills, Brighouse & Rastrick, YEWCO Works (this new band contained some members from the famous St Hilda Colliery Band, which disbanded in 1937), Crossley Carpets, Carlton Main Frickley Colliery, Butterfield's Tank Works and Markham Main Colliery. I was absolutely overawed by their musicality and technical brilliance. Incidentally, Black Dyke's principal cornet player that day was the young, brilliant Maurice Murphy, who later became a legend in his own lifetime as a soloist and as principal trumpet in a long career with the London Symphony Orchestra. Lance Wynn, from the Northeast of England, occupied the solo trombone chair before moving to the John White Footwear Band. Lance was my hero then – I often wonder what became of him.

Brass bands then had a reputation as hard drinking outfits. Some were like that, but drink had no place on the contest platform. Conductor George insisted on total abstinence until the band had played. This was more than mild torture if we'd been unlucky with the draw and had to wait hours before our turn to perform. However, the respect for George and the players' dedication was such that I can't ever remember anyone breaking the rule. After playing – well, that was a very different matter. I had my first drink shortly after I joined the band. Phillip bought it for me on condition I didn't tell my Dad. I did enjoy a beer or two and even the odd whisky from time to time. I vowed that because Mum and Dad had trusted me with a house key to let myself in, often in the small hours of the morning, I'd never return home seriously worse for wear. Mum and Dad must have realised that I had started drinking, underage of course, but never passed comment.

From the band we also formed a trombone quartet, again for contest purposes. Alan Thomas played first trombone, I played second, Stuart Gill from Skelmanthorpe Band guested on third with Phillip Hallas bass trombone. Horn player, Alf Haigh was the conductor and our speciality was *Comrades in Arms*. Quartet contests and solo slow melody contests too were very popular then and were often held in working men's clubs as Saturday evening entertainment. Our first successes were contests at Silkstone and Spring Vale clubs where we won hands down. The most serious and prestigious quartet contest was at Holmebridge. At that venue we never managed to beat a superb trombone quartet from Scotland's John Fauld's Works Band led by the talented player, George Gilmour. These quartet contests allowed any combination of 4 brass instruments and some pretty unusual and, in many ways amusing, outfits turned up – 4 basses, 4 horns,

2 cornets and 2 trombones for example, although the most popular choice was 2 cornets, horn and euphonium.

I'd made good progress in the band without specialist tuition and several players suggested to my Dad that I would benefit from private lessons from a specialist trombone teacher. I'm not sure how it was arranged, but I was taken under Grenville Richmond's wing at Brighouse and Rastrick. Although Grenville was still in his 20's, he had been solo trombone with this famous band for some years, having himself been a pupil of the respected teacher, Ernest Appleyard. I travelled every Saturday morning to have my lesson at Grenville's parents' house in Rastrick and looked forward eagerly to the experience. Grenville taught by example and with him I progressed by leaps and bounds.

After a while he thought I would perform well in slow melody contests. These events always drew large entries, with up to 40 in each class. Usually there was a junior class (with an upper age limit of 18 years), which often commenced as early as 1pm. After tea, the open section usually got under way at 6pm and often didn't finish until around 10pm, such were the number of entries. Cornet players were in the majority closely followed by those performing on horn and euphonium. Playing the trombone, at least I gave the unseen adjudicator a welcome change from listening to an almost unbroken stream of the popular favourites; *The Holy City* and *The Lost Chord*. For slow melody contests, the pieces I studied with Grenville were *Nirvana, Lend Me Your Aid* and my particular favourite, *Where 'ere You Walk*. In contrast to my dislike of violin competitions, I found these occasions very enjoyable and there was a friendly atmosphere amongst listeners and competitors alike. My best result was at Marsden Mechanics Institute where I won the junior event in the afternoon and on the same day came second in the evening's open event, both with *Where 'ere You Walk* – I only wish I'd kept the adjudicator's remarks.

Although I was still playing 2nd trombone at Clayton West, by now bands in higher sections were becoming interested in signing me, some offering the first trombone chair. I was sorely tempted to go, but a reshuffle in the band with Alan Thomas moving to euphonium allowed me to move up to solo trombone. I enjoyed the responsibility and for concerts I was expected to play either one or perhaps two solos. The flashy numbers I chose were *The Acrobat* and *The Joker* whilst my slow melodies were *Where 'ere You Walk, Angels Guard Thee* and *Panis Angelicus.*

Myself in civies ready to set off for a solo performance, 1955 Boosey & Hawkes Imperial trombone with low pitch tuning slide

From time to time I was also approached to play solos in variety concerts mainly in church and chapel halls. One of the more memorable concerts was in a chapel hall at Higham, on the outskirts of Barnsley. I was expected, along with the other performers, to do my turn surrounded by a wooden frame about 3 feet square suspended by long strings from the ceiling. The frame was supposed to represent a television screen, TV being in its infancy and quite a novelty then. The singers and other performers had no problem in meeting this bizarre request. For me it was not so simple as I was expected to face obliquely through the frame with the trombone slide poking through. Several times I managed to catch the frame edge with the slide, which set the whole contraption swinging wildly and in danger of collapse.

In those days bands played on so-called high pitch instruments with A at 456 Hertz, a hang-over from Victorian times. Tuning the trombone to a piano which, like orchestras, was technically tuned to concert pitch (often referred to as low pitch) with A at 440 Hertz could be a chancy business. The piano only had to be a shade flat to require the trombone tuning slide to be pulled out so far it was in danger of dropping out. Several times when doing my solo I could hear a soft buzzing sound behind my left ear due to a slight escape of air past the over-extended tuning slide. Mum and Dad unexpectedly solved this problem by buying me a brand new Boosey & Hawkes Imperial trombone in high pitch, but importantly, it came complete with an additional low pitch tuning slide. I knew absolutely nothing of their planned generous gesture. It was only when they returned from holiday in Southsea that they revealed they had stopped off at Boosey & Hawkes shop in London's Regent Street and ordered it on the spot. I was absolutely dumbstruck, but so excited that I could hardly wait for its delivery at Clayton West railway station about a week later. This instrument retailed for £52-10s-0d (£52.50), a sizeable sum in those days. The new trombone had a larger bore than the old small bore 'pea-shooters' that I'd played so far. Consequently the tone was mellow and ringing but far less hard and strident than the old instruments. It was easy to blow and the slide action was light making this new trombone a joy to play.

The end of my full time membership of Clayton West Band was forced upon me soon after I started work at Park Mill Colliery. I was working underground and was also committed to attending Barnsley Technical College. My academic workload was a heavy one as I had determined that I wanted, ultimately, to study at university and winning a scholarship was vital. One complete day on paid release from work together with 3 evenings per week was the demanding technical college schedule. In addition, there was always set homework to be completed, so attendance at regular band practices was out of the question. I did continue to play with the band on occasional engagements including the odd contest – even the National Finals in London some years later.

News soon travelled round the brass band world that I was no longer full time at Clayton West and for quite a long period the house was besieged by band secretaries attempting to sign me. Laurence Mann, Skelmanthorpe's band secretary and a class bass trombonist (later with Carlton Main Frickley Colliery) was particularly persuasive. Of course, full time commitment was out of the question, but having my own instrument allowed me to freelance with many bands including Skelmanthorpe, Emley, Flockton, Woolley Colliery, Hade Edge, Honley, Royston New Monkton Colliery and Carlton Main Frickley Colliery. At this time, my wardrobe at home contained a selection of uniforms lent by the various bands. On one occasion I had no fewer than 5 uniforms stowed away and not one of them was anywhere near a decent fit! At several contests I'll admit that I appeared illegally and signed the name of players registered with those bands. The original test pieces, which gave me the greatest thrill were *Lorenzo, Coriolanus, Labour and Love, The Three Musketeers,* along with the transcriptions of Lizst's *Les Preludes, The Works of Mendelssohn* and Berlioz's *Les Franc Juges.* These pieces I found exciting, but very demanding, as I didn't have many rehearsals to prepare.

Myself in the uniform of Skelmanthorpe Band
1953

Playing with so many bands gave me an early rare insight into the mysterious world of conducting. For me, the most terrifying character was the old warhorse Noel Thorpe, who in 1938 had taken Slaithwaite Band to the very pinnacle of success with their win in the British Open Championship at Belle Vue. He had a ferocious temper if things weren't to his liking and a withering look could reduce the stoutest of players to a shaking jelly. Amongst the other conductors I remember were Willie Kaye (no relation to my former violin teacher) at Skelmanthorpe, Charlie Westerby (formerly solo cornet with Brighouse & Rastrick) at Flockton and Albert Robinson at Hade Edge. Albert was one of the old school of conductors who wore an out-of-fashion bandmasters black 'frock' coat with a high collar and dark red sash round the midriff. On the platform he always carried his cornet in his right hand. This allowed him to 'bump up' the solo cornets in a forte tutti passage. He had to turn the pages of the musical score with his left hand consequently he didn't use a baton. He had lost his own front teeth and in order for him to blow the cornet it was rumoured that he himself had fashioned a special false set from gutta-percha. Despite my work, study and freelance banding commitments I still found time for the occasional private lesson with Grenville Richmond at Brighouse and Rastrick and eventually had the opportunity to play engagements with that band when Bill Beverley, their 2nd trombone was ill for a period.

Playing in brass bands wasn't always deadly serious and there were many amusing incidents. One, I remember well, concerned Sid Orr, an Eflat bass player with Clayton West band, which at the time had just received a new set of 4 basses from the Coal Industry Welfare Organisation (CISWO). The first outing for the new instruments was a Saturday open-air concert in Normanton Park. That day Sid blew his heart out, but the instrument's response was feeble, to say the least. This lack of 'oomph' worried Sid all weekend, for he assumed that he had inadvertently damaged the instrument in some way. However, he confided in no-one. On the following Monday he mentioned to his wife that she had forgotten to provide the customary sandwiches. She replied that she had put them, as usual, down the large bell of the bass for easy transportation. An immediate search and shaking of the instrument revealed they had passed right around the first bend and lodged inside the instrument out of sight. No wonder the bass produced hardly a grunt! Needless to say, the retrieval of the now stale sandwiches made Sid a very relieved man indeed.

Writing of bass players reminds me of Sid's colleague, Bflat bass player Wilf Addy. Wilf was built like a house, standing well over 6 feet tall and weighing in at approaching 20 stones – he made the massive Bflat bass look like a cornet in his hands. Wilf, a former euphoniumist, was an excellent player and capable of a feat, which I'm sure only he could achieve. If he felt peckish during a performance he'd produce a pork pie from his pocket, take a great bite of it during a couple of bars rest, then continue playing.

What the interior of his instrument must have been like doesn't bear thinking about!

The only time I've been a percussionist ended in ignominious failure, much to the amusement of other band members. Clayton West band always toured the village playing carols on Christmas Day and Boxing Day. A stop at The Woodman pub, with landlord Billy Hawke providing a round of free drinks, and later stops at The Junction and The Shoulder of Mutton pubs together with drinks provided at several houses on our travels ensured that by mid afternoon most players were feeling slightly unsteady. One Boxing Day, at a halt in High Street, our bass drummer, blacksmith Bert Swanwick, needed to leave the scene for necessary relief. I took over the bass drum duty. Even though it was mid-afternoon, *Hail Smiling Morn* was a popular request. It is a rousing 6/8 melody, which allowed me ample opportunity to show off my newly acquired bass drum skills. By the second verse, my confidence was high and I was now belting the drum hard at 2 beats to the bar when, to my absolute horror, I lost my grip on the drumstick. I could only look anxiously as it described a beautiful arc through the air and disappeared under a passing No.15 Yorkshire Traction double decker bus on its way to Barnsley. Much to my relief, it wasn't smashed to matchwood under the wheels, nor had it lodged on the bus's underside to end up in Barnsley bus station. I put the drum down on the road and made off to recover the stick only to find the drum rolling away down the hill. I sprinted off after the run-away drum and caught it just before it mounted the pavement, thus preventing it smashing into a stone wall. Sheepishly, I returned to recover the stick, realising in a flash that percussionists must be the kamikazes of the musical world.

Although the drumstick incident was embarrassing enough for me, it pales into insignificance compared to my absolute faux pas at a Belle Vue contest. I can't even remember the test piece, but I must have had a temporary loss of concentration and managed to play a forte middle C, about a crotchet's worth in fact, in a silent bar. The note, right in the middle of the trombone's range, echoed around the hushed hall. How I wished the floor would open up and swallow me! I know I'm not the first, nor will I be the last to commit this cardinal sin, which is known in the musical trade as 'playing a domino'. That dreadful error was undoubtedly the most embarrassing moment in a musical career of over 60 years.

In the early 1950's I'd also become very interested in jazz and dance music. I listened whenever possible to BBC's Jazz Club broadcast early on Saturday evening and I was an avid reader of the long established Melody Maker and the upstart New Musical Express. Although modern jazz and beepop was being developed, jazz bands were mainly playing so-called traditional jazz. The most popular bands were led by Humphrey Lyttleton, Joe Daniels, Freddie Randall, Sid Phillips and Mick Mulligan along with outfits such as the Crane River Jazz band and the Avon City Stompers – Chris Barber hadn't yet appeared on the scene. The ballroom dancing craze was still going strong and big bands, playing mainly swing numbers, broadcast regularly from the large dance halls such as the Hammersmith Palais and the Tower Ballroom, Blackpool. These excellent bands were led by the likes of Ted Heath, Joe Loss, Geraldo, Ken Mackintosh and Kenny Baker. I was absolutely astounded by the technical brilliance of dance band musicians. The range, dexterity and superb tone of trombonists like Don Lusher and George Chisholm left most brass band trombonists standing. Of course, the skills of those playing in local dance bands, which were usually much smaller outfits than the big bands, were hardly those of the superb professionals, but nevertheless, most were excellent musicians.

I did my first dance band playing whilst still at Penistone Grammar School. A school friend, John Fisher, an accomplished dance band pianist, was already leading a small band, sadly, the name of which now escapes me. The band rehearsed at Dogley Lane chapel schoolroom in Kirkburton. The existing line-up was 2 saxes, trumpet, and piano with another Penistonian, Lambert Halstead, on drums. The only other member I recall was a chap called George Tricket on trumpet, who seemed ancient, but was probably only in his 40's. John invited me to join and I had the shock of my life when I attended my first rehearsal to discover that the trombone parts were all in the bass clef – a complete mystery to me. I felt such a fool that I was unable to sight read in this clef and I hardly blew a note during the 2 hour rehearsal. I took the parts away and worked at them furiously so that I was able to make a decent showing at my first engagement with the band few days later – effectively I played my first job without rehearsal. The band played for dances mainly around the Huddersfield area and so I was returned home by taxi, the 'Last Waltz' of Saturday evening dances being timed to finish at 11.30pm.

One engagement I remember well was at Kirkheaton, on the outskirts of Huddersfield. The hall was a decent size but the stage was far too narrow to accommodate the band in comfort. I was sitting at the front of the stage with the saxes and trumpet to my left and the piano and drums behind. The only way I could squeeze on was to have two beer crates supporting the outer legs of my chair. As the band members stamped their feet (dance band players were prone to do that) the stage began swaying and the gap between the stage and the crates gradually widened and I felt in danger of falling through. At the end of each set I had to jump off the stage and reset the beer crates.

My next dance band, The Skyliners, was a far more professional affair. It was run by alto sax player, Stuart Ferguson, from Skelmanthorpe. Stuart, was an excellent all-round musician and a superb trombonist too, who I first met in the Skelmanthorpe Band. He had also played with Woolley Colliery Band and a short period with Morris Motors Band. The Skyliners could put on a big band performance with up to 16 or so players, but the numbers were variable depending upon the nature of the engagement. At busy times, such as Christmas and the New Year, the band often split into two, with extra personnel being brought in to fill specific vacancies. The regular rhythm section was pianist Eddie Wray, drummer Ron Bowker and bassist Gilbert Pell. Other popular band members were Peter Fretwell on trumpet, Stuart Gill on trombone and Arnold Wood on baritone sax.

One incident with this band sticks in my memory. We had been engaged to play a gig at Ryhill, out in the country near Wakefield. The band members travelled in convoy in 2 taxis. Passing Woolley Hall Training College in pitch darkness, the second taxi broke down and its demise was not spotted by anyone in the leading car, which proceeded to the venue. I was in the leading car along with several other players, but none of the rhythm section. At the hall we took our time setting up, awaiting the arrival of the second car. By the time the dance was scheduled to start, there was no sign of the other band members and it was obvious to us that something was amiss. The organiser was becoming concerned at our prevarication and eventually somewhat agitated. Finally we had to appease him and make a start with a bizarre combination of instruments. Some half hour later, the reinforcements arrived, having been picked up by our taxi retracing its route to base.

It was in this band that I took my first tentative steps as a double bass player. Gilbert, knowing that I'd played the fiddle, taught me the basics of pizzicato bass in a few spare moments. Gilbert had quite an eye for the ladies and if he spotted a potential date he'd go off and chat her up during a number where my trombone part wasn't that critical so I could then fill in for him on bass. Crucially, Gilbert's bass technique hadn't moved into the 20th century for he was still playing on an old 3 string bass tuned in 5ths. It was only later when I got an instrument of my own that I discovered basses had 4 strings tuned in 4ths, so all my earlier labours, in terms of learning the instrument, had been to no avail. I have often wondered whether Gilbert's bass was made by a famous maker and whether it would have been any good for orchestral work – in its favour, it was certainly at the latest a 19th century instrument.

Although I moved into orchestral playing some years later, first with the trombone then later with the double bass, what I had learnt in brass bands laid the foundations for a long career in this most demanding of disciplines. But, more than that, my time in brass bands gave me tremendous enjoyment and great enthusiasm for music making. I count myself lucky to have stumbled, by chance, into this wonderful movement.

11
GOOGLIES, GURGLES, GIRLS AND GOD

There's no doubt about it – I could have opened the batting for England if only they'd played test matches with a tennis ball. Put me on a proper cricket square facing a fast bowler with a leather cased 'corkie', my first instinct was to get myself out and back into the safety of the pavilion. In my defence, I can testify that the village cricket wickets I played on were temperamental beasts and it was well nigh impossible to predict the flight of the ball after it had pitched. The batsman of those days, with but sparse body protection and long before the advent of protective helmets, really was on a hiding to nothing. One delivery would scream past at head height and still rising, causing the wicketkeeper to perform an athletic upward leap to stop 4 byes. The next ball would be a 'shooter' and scurry under the raised bat, an off target delivery being the batsman's only hope of surviving dismissal.

Cricket, along with soccer to a lesser extent, were the main sporting activities in the Upper Dearne Valley. Organised soccer teams tended to be populated by young men in a relatively narrow age band, players coming into the team at about 17 years of age and retiring when reaching their mid 30's. Few village soccer clubs ran a reserve team in which the youngsters could participate. Cricket, on the other hand, had a much wider appeal within the communities with all the village clubs running a second team and often a junior side as well. In consequence, boys were often playing in the second team as young as 13 years old, just as I was with Nortonthorpe Cricket Club. It was not uncommon for men in their 50's, having served their time in the first team to return to guide the up and coming youngsters in the 2nd eleven. Furthermore, it was a game where all family members became involved, with mums, wives and girlfriends initially coming along as spectators and ending up making and serving teas between the innings.

I've heard it said that every father in Yorkshire hoped that his son would be born with a cricket bat in one hand and a copy of Handel's Messiah in the other. As far as I'm aware, no such miraculous birth has ever occurred, but I can appreciate the sentiment. Certainly for me, I started playing cricket at about 3 years old with Dad bowling underarm at me on granddad Hellewell's lawn. As the years passed, I certainly went through a few cricket sets with the bats growing bigger each time. At junior school we played cricket in the yard with the wickets chalked on the wall. Of course, with the absence of bails, one can readily imagine the disputes, which regularly arose regarding dismissals. Many times the rubber ball was forensically examined by the fielding side for the slightest speck of chalk dust in the hope of convincing proof that the batsman had been bowled out. Usually no such evidence could be evinced and a sporting occasion degenerated into shouting match at best and often into a bout of fisticuffs.

I was probably 10 or 11 years old when I first joined Nortonthorpe Cricket Club as a junior member. Once again, the name of the club indicates the immense influence that the Norton family held in Scissett. The ground was at the top of Springfield Avenue and hadn't long been established there. The field was steeply sloping and a poorly levelled cricket square had simply been excavated into the hillside. Fielders on the down slope side of the square soon became disheartened, for even the feeblest of shots into that area rapidly picked up speed and scurried across the boundary for 4 runs. By way of compensation, many a powerful drive up the slope slowed so dramatically that a certain looking 4 could be cut off by a jubilant fielder. The pavilion, a purpose built white painted wooden structure was situated at the top of the slope and afforded an excellent, almost bird's eye view of proceedings, particularly from the scorer's box. This was no consolation for visiting teams who, rightly, considered the ground by far the worst in the Huddersfield Central League.

An early game of cricket on granddad
Hellewell's lawn at Kitchenroyd, 1939

The club didn't run a junior team, but that omission simply encouraged the younger members to show some initiative and issue challenges to groups of lads from surrounding villages. These challenge matches were often played on a home and away basis and were usually quite enjoyable events. My contribution was as a batsman and wicketkeeper – as a bowler I was hopeless. I tried spin bowling, but sadly my leg breaks were easily spotted and usually dispatched to the boundary. I tried googlies but they were absolutely dire. My pace bowling was best described as mediocre, lacking both pace and direction. The wicketkeeping role I thoroughly enjoyed and through practice I became pretty adept. I enjoyed being involved with every ball, rather than standing out in the field waiting for something to happen. One beautiful summer evening I remember playing a match at Clayton West's pretty and compact ground and taking 5 catches, probably my best ever performance.

Of course, I never played for England at cricket, nor for that matter any other sport, but I can well imagine the feelings a player has when receiving that first 'call-up'. In my case I was 13 years old and I'll never forget how proud and excited I was to see my name on the Nortonthorpe CC 2nd XI team sheet displayed in the Conservative Club window for all the world to see. Never mind that I was down at No. 11 and that it was August when some regulars were off on holiday. I'd made it into a proper adult team! It was an away match against Lepton Highlanders. For days I was on cloud 9, but this excitement was tinged with a little apprehension and, if truth to tell, dread, that the opposition would unleash some demon fast bowler.

Travelling to away matches was an experience in itself. No luxury coach, simply Sandy Haigh's coal lorry, which had been swept out for the occasion and covered with a rough tarpaulin tent-like structure. We'd already changed into our whites at home – my kit coming courtesy of Arthur Batty, who'd now retired from the game. Our cricket boots were tied together by the laces and slung around our necks – no posh sports bags back then. It really was a feat to clamber up into the back of the lorry, whilst at the same time avoiding coal dust soiling our pristine whites. Throughout the 20 minute journey we were rocked, jolted and many times in danger of being thrown off the two wooden side benches and onto the floor. The talk during the entire journey, I remember, was about a serious matter – cricket, both local and county, such was the enthusiasm and dedication of these amateur players.

My recollections of the game as a whole are very sparse, although I remember that we won the toss and batted first. This ensured that, barring an unlikely big stand somewhere in our innings and a consequent declaration, I would have to bat. Before long my time came. All padded up and with words of encouragement from my captain, Ernest Bentley, I strode out to the wicket, my fake bravado attempting to conceal a dreadful dose of nerves. My friend, Garth (yes, him again) was at the non-striker's end. Once at the wicket it wasn't so daunting and from the umpire I took my usual middle and leg guard. I do remember my short innings in some detail. The previous batsman had been dismissed on the third ball of the over and so I had the remaining three balls to face. The first of these from a medium pace bowler I played at and missed, but fortunately I didn't get a touch. The next ball I played straight back down the pitch to be fielded by the bowler. The last ball of the over I contrived to middle and it rocketed off into the covers for a single. Feeling much relieved and now full of confidence, I now faced a fast bowler from the other end. Discretion got the better of me and I took a wild swing at his first delivery, totally misjudged the pace, with the result that I heard the dreaded clatter of the stumps being shattered. At least I'd broken my duck in my first league game!

Despite the rather feeble showing in my first match, I continued to be selected for the remainder of the season and somehow managed to complete a few innings with totals into double figures. One match I remember well, was an evening encounter against Emley held on consecutive days at their ground and remarkable for the ferocity of the opposition brace of fast bowlers. Trevor and Tony Booth (not related) were proper tearaways on the pitch and weren't averse to slinging down a couple of bouncers followed by a full toss aimed at the body. I'll never forget facing Tony Booth, a thick set lad with a mop of ginger hair. His enormous long runs were enough to frighten most batsmen and he put so much effort into his delivery I'm sure he felt cheated if he didn't take a wicket with every ball. I'd managed to stonewall his first four deliveries, which didn't put him in a friendly frame of mind. The next ball was a Yorker, which went under my bat and struck my big toe an excruciating blow. The last ball of the over was a full toss aimed at the body, which with no skill on my part actually hit the top of my bat handle and flew upwards, beating the fielder on the third man boundary for a 4. Tony was not best pleased, but he didn't have the satisfaction of taking my wicket, which I lost giving a dolly catch to a slow bowler George William Scargill, who some years later became my boss in work for a short period.

From the outset of the next season I was a regular choice as a batsman for Nortonthorpe's 2nd XI. Very early in the season I remember playing a match at the pretty Holmbridge ground in the shadow of the mighty Holme Moss. The thermometer was near to freezing point and the outfield covered with a light sprinkling of snow. As the summer wore on clashes began to occur with Saturday engagements of Clayton West Band, of which I was now a member. It became apparent that I couldn't do justice to both and I recall the band conductor, George Hallas, speaking to me quite earnestly and telling me that I would have to make a choice. In all fairness he didn't try to persuade me to give up cricket, but I rather fancy that he knew where my loyalty would lie. Thus ended my short league cricket career.

Memory can play strange and disconcerting tricks, but I've no recollection whatsoever of a time when I couldn't swim. In some ways that's not surprising bearing in mind that a half a mile walk from home brought me to a magnificent 25yard, 4 lane heated indoor swimming pool. I know of no other village in the country, which sixty plus years ago could boast such a marvellous aquatic centre. How's that for luck? How is it that a village with a population of less than 2000 came to possess such a rare sporting facility? Did some rich benefactor donate the money? No, it was down entirely to the local miners who contributed to the Miner's Welfare Fund from their weekly wages. Apparently they were given the choice of either pithead baths in which to shower after their shift or a swimming baths to serve the local community. Unselfishly they chose the latter. By serendipity, the grandly named Clayton West and Emley Miners Welfare Swimming Baths was built at Scissett and opened in 1929.

My early memories of gurgling around in the water have long since faded, although I can remember making my first forays from the shallow end and finishing up, well out of my depth, at the deep end. I cannot be sure how old I was when I first went to the baths, but remember being taken by Richard White, a boy some 5 years older than myself -- it's even likely I hadn't even started school. In those early days Mr Bell was the baths manager, who I remember retiring and being replaced towards the end of the war by Mr Lewis Calvert.

Ladies had a very raw deal indeed in terms of the pool time. Of the available sessions, mixed bathing was permitted on Tuesday and Saturday afternoons and Thursday afternoon was ladies only. Every other session was limited to men!! The admission cost appears incredibly cheap by today's standards, which in truth it was. A junior card cost 2 shillings (10p), and this not for one session's swim, but for a whole season! After a few years this was raised to 2s 6d (12.5p), which almost caused a riot. The actual cost was still an absolute bargain but we viewed the 25% increase as unreasonable. The small folding printed admission card was divided into the appropriate number of swimming weeks with a grid of six squares per week. This was presented at the turnstile entrance and the attendance marked with a pencil cross. In theory, only one swimming session per day was allowed, but many times after a morning swim lads used to erase the pencil cross and reappear for the afternoon or evening session. The swimming season ran from May until the end of September. During the school term I'd swim at least 3 times a week, walking the 200 yards across the Brick Field straight after school. In the school holidays this would often increase to 5 or 6 times a week.

Lads being lads, often we weren't all that well behaved. The baths manager, lumbered with every job around the place, didn't have much time supervise the pool. Supervision, when it did happen, was nothing more than an occasional visit to peer through the double doors at the shallow end and make sure nobody had managed to drown themselves. This gave us ample opportunity to get up to all manner of tricks. However, anyone unlucky enough to be caught misbehaving would be given their marching orders and suspended for a week. There was a diving board at the deep end, the top board, I would guess, was about 12 feet above the water surface. A favourite pastime, 'bombing', although frowned upon, was simply to jump off the top board holding the knees and aim to land about a foot or so away from some unfortunate individual swimming below. I remember on one occasion misjudging my leap and catching my friend, John Booth, a glancing blow in the small of the back. He was in pain for some while, but fortunately recovered without serious damage being inflicted.

Another, very dangerous trick was to shin up to the balcony, stand on the balcony rail and catch hold of one of the steel roof trusses. From there we'd swing hand over hand along the truss until we were positioned directly over the pool and then simply let go from that enormous height. On other occasions we would dive into the water from the top of the balcony rail. Although I'd performed this feat many times, one attempt almost landed me with a very serious accident. My wet foot slipped as I dived off the rail and my trajectory was such I didn't clear the bath side some 20 feet below. Fortunately, it was only my feet, which hit the edge of the pool and, although these were severely bruised, no lasting damage was done. I did, however, on one occasion manage to break a toe, which was never properly reset and through life I've carried this crooked souvenir as a reminder of those happy times.

Dearne Valley Swimming Club was a feature of local life. This had been founded in 1931 and afforded the opportunity for boys and young men of the district (in actual fact drawn mainly from Scissett, Clayton West and Denby Dale) to take part in competitive events. The main focus of the club was water polo, a rather vicious and exhausting game. The club competed in a league of about 8 teams drawn mainly from Yorkshire's heavy woollen district. Although I never played water polo competitively, I remember travelling to baths in Lockwood, Cleckheaton, Batley and Heckmondwike as a member of Dearne Valley's junior squadron racing team. The competitive Friday evening fixtures always opened with the squadron races before going on to the main event – the polo match. Home matches always drew a capacity attendance with spectators occupying seats in the balcony and temporary seating at the pool side. Water polo is an ideal game for dirty players and on many occasions the local partisan crowd was not averse to prolonged bouts of booing and verbal abuse at the underhand tactics of opposition players.

Of course, our men gave as good as they got and loud cheers would ring out when an opponent was dragged under water. My several years of enjoyable club membership came to an end when once again Friday night band practice took priority.

The baths also formed the focus of a well loved and popular winter distraction. During the cold months the pool was drained and a superb sprung wooden dance floor was laid. The complex wooden structure, which filled the bath void and supported the floor, was a real work of art and a credit to Burton's joinery in Clayton West who had designed and constructed the whole project. Every Saturday evening throughout winter, dances were held. These events were extremely well supported and not only attracted the locals but also drew crowds of young people from quite a wide area. The dance and a whist drive, which was held for the older patrons in the balcony, always commenced at 7.30pm. Few young people bothered to turn up for the start of dancing, this group usually arriving from around 8.30pm onward, many often having visited one of the local pubs or the adjacent Scissett Working Men's Club. An interval of at least half an hour, to give the live band a breather, usually took place shortly after the end of the whist drive, say around 9.00pm.

The evening's dancing was very well organised and controlled by the evening dress clad resident MC, Ronnie Bentley. Ronnie, incidentally, ran dancing classes in Scissett Parish Room and like all local lads and lassies I learned to dance at quite a young age, although I must admit that this social skill is now rather rusty. The dances were always run in sets of 3 with the Quickstep, the Foxtrot and the Waltz being the most frequent and popular. Immediately after the interval there would be an 'Old Time' set comprising the Gay Gordons, the Military 2 Step and the Viennese Waltz and somewhere during the evening there would be a Latin American set – considered in those days a rather daring innovation. The bands were of variable musicality, proficiency and composition, with a line up of 2 trumpets, 2 saxes, piano and drums being the most frequent. Dance band personnel, with the exception of Mrs Bond from Sunnymead, who led a peculiar combination on the piano accordion, was entirely male dominated.

Attending dances from quite a young age brought me into social contact with girls for the first time, meeting them in the school environment could hardly be classed as social. Naturally, like all lads, I was at first rather awkward and shy about chatting to girls and, in particular, asking them to dance. After a while, however, I gained confidence and after spotting a nice looking girl dressed up in her finery I would leave my mates to go over to chat her up. This seemed the most natural thing in the world.

There were many lovely girls not only from Scissett and the immediate surrounding villagers of Skelmanthorpe, Denby Dale, Clayton West and Emley, but the lasses from the Barnsley side, Darton, Kexborough and Mapplewell seemed to me extremely attractive. Many of the latter travelled over each day to work in Beanland's or Teddy Blackburn's mills so they were familiar with the district and thought they may as well play here as well as work here. Naturally enough, casual friendships developed into more lasting, though still somewhat transient relationships. Throughout my teens I had a series of girl friends, all of whom at the time I was quite serious about initially. Relationships break up for all manner of reasons and it was quite common to hear variations of the expression *he/she has been chucked.* It was similar to stepping on and off a carousel as the partners of a broken relationship soon tagged up with someone else.

Of course, it became known amongst the lads who amongst the girls could be classed as *hot stuff.* Many girls were not averse to leaving the dance and going out for at least a kiss and cuddle in the darkness of Tipler's Lane, which ran alongside the baths. It was not uncommon to walk past half a dozen or so couples so engaged to find a quiet spot for ones own amorous pursuits. As the title of the book suggests, I did from time to time get lucky. It is always said that the sexual revolution in Britain was in the swinging 60's. Whilst this may have been true for London, a mild form of this revolution had certainly arrived in my part of Yorkshire some 10 years earlier!

Sex education for us was non-existent – parents of my generation were simply too embarrassed to discuss it with their children and this topic in schools was still many years away. Sex manuals hadn't yet seen the light of day, or if they had they hadn't reached the Upper Dearne Valley. We had to content ourselves with avidly reading whatever ragged, dog-eared salacious novel was in current circulation. It was almost by a process of osmosis that we acquired our knowledge from hearing older lads talk, but one can well imagine the mass of duff information resulting from this informal method. Whilst both lads and lassies were keen to experience the pleasure, which close bodily contact can bring, their enthusiasm was tempered by lack of opportunity and the fact that effective birth control methods were, for us, limited. Parents didn't often go out, cars for us were a few years away and the near freezing temperature outdoors in winter was usually enough to dampen all but the most determined couple's efforts. Of course, summer in the fields and woods was rather a different matter, but in winter the best hope was on the back row of the double seats in Skelmanthorpe's Savoy cinema.

The only available birth control was the condom, always referred to by the lads as the 'Rubber Johnny' or 'French Letter'. This essential commodity was sometimes in short supply. It would have been too embarrassing for us to buy them in the village's chemist shop, for the proprietor, Clifford Thomson, had known us all since we were small boys. Strategic supplies, however, were bought from a small barber's shop in Market Hill, Barnsley. The fear of an unwanted pregnancy was, for the girl, a strong deterrent and many a passionate encounter was brought to an abrupt end, much to the lad's disappointment.

The desire for conquest was always there amongst the lads, but we always respected the girl's wishes. I certainly never heard of one sexual attack or rape. I believe that we had a wholesome approach to sexual matters such that it was safe for girls to walk

152

home at night from dances or the pictures along dark lonely roads.

There was, occasionally, one aspect of the dances, which could be threatening at times, even if one was not directly involved. A gang of lads from a particular village would deliberately pick a fight with lads from elsewhere. Rarely did violence break out in the hall, but along Wakefield Road at the end of the dance there could be mayhem with 30 or 40 lads involved. The occasional knife was flashed, but in the main fighting was confined to fists. This was the 'Teddy Boy' era when lads sported Elvis type hairdos, huge sideburns and their attire consisted of long jackets, often with velvet lapels, drainpipe trousers, bootlace or painted ties and thick crepe soled shoes, known as brothel creepers. This era was the precursor of the mods and rockers fights of a decade later and what we now see happening between sets of rival football supporters.

God – or to be more precise his representative in Scissett, The Church of England, had a profound effect on my early life. Realistically, I hadn't a choice. Scissett was an island of mild conservatism in politics and theology surrounded as it was by the forces of radicalism and nonconformity. St. Augustine's, a Waterloo church dating from 1839 was one of a large number established around that time to serve the country's burgeoning industrial population and was the sole place of worship in the village. Any inhabitant wishing to depart from the established orthodoxy had to travel to surrounding villages to exercise that choice. Those so minded faced a dilemma with a myriad of options. Congregationalists, Baptists, Primitive Methodists (known locally as The Ranters or The Prims), Wesleyan Methodists, Methodist New Connexion, Salvationists and other splinter factions competed in the business of saving souls. Amazingly, the contiguous village of Clayton West boasted no fewer than 7 nonconformist chapels. Incidentally, the chapels in that village didn't get it all their own way for there were an equal number of pubs, and all for a population of something around 2000! I often used to wonder why nonconformism had never taken root in Scissett, for all the ingredients were apparently in place. In later life I came to realise the immense influence, which the all-powerful Norton family exercised in 'their' village. I'm certain that the family's commitment to the low-church Anglican cause was sufficient to frighten off any aspiring rival theology.

I cannot claim that youngsters in the village were in any sense deeply religious and they certainly were not pious, but the majority of us, except those from the tiny minority non-conformist families, became involved in the church in some way or other. It was, I suppose, akin to young Germans joining the Hitler Jugend[1] (HJ) or the Bund Deutsche Maedchen[1] (BDM). It was expected of us and, like membership of the HJ or the BDM in the early days, our involvement with activities of the church was also exciting and enjoyable. Furthermore we were part of a coherent group and this sense of belonging was undoubtedly an important psychological factor – an individual simply didn't want to be left outside the action. These reasons were sufficient for many children whose parents were not regular churchgoers to gravitate to the church.

My parents were committed Anglicans and soon I was taken along to morning service, which in those days was always Matins – sung Eucharist was many years away. Dad being absent from home for much of the war, the duty fell to Mum. I can remember that I didn't care much for the service and I disliked intensely the continual standing up, sitting down and kneeling routine, much preferring instead to sit still and look at the lovely stained glass windows. Mum kept hinting that I ought to attend Sunday School, but I learned that this would involve being there some 45 minutes earlier and so I managed to resist this by pretending to enjoy the service.

I was about 8 years old when I became a probationer in the choir. This was the first time I was mixing with boys who were much older than myself, many being 13 or 14 years of age — boys voices seemed to break later in those days. Incidentally, girl choristers were anathema then! The choir was like a secret club and probationers had to undergo initiation ceremonies, including being locked in the pitch-black, cobweb filled 'Dragon Hole' underneath the chancel. This housed the electric bellows to pump the organ and it could be a terrifying place for an incarcerated young 8 year old, particularly when the bellows started operating.

The choirmaster was Mr Charlesworth, who had recently taken over from old Tom Morley, who had given a lifetime's service in that role - my Dad was a chorister under him. Being so young, I had no way of judging Mr Charlesworth's musical competence as a choir trainer and organist. He was, however, a kind well-meaning person, but totally lacked the ability to control an unruly set of boys. For sheer devilment, our escapades before and after choir practice belied our angelic appearance on Sundays when we were garbed in purple cassock, nicely ironed white surplice and topped off with a white ruffle.

The practices were scheduled to start at 7pm on Wednesdays and Fridays, but I can't remember that ambitious target ever being met. We would deliberately arrive early and hide ourselves in remote places all over the church. On one occasion Mr Charlesworth became so frustrated he took a flying kick at a body crouched under the pulpit. Poor Melvin Lodge was the recipient – nowadays there would be the inevitable court case, but then Melvin knew that he himself was in the wrong and took the punishment without complaint. It was usually 10 minutes or so after the scheduled start by the time Mr Charlesworth had coaxed us into the choir stalls with a mixture of threats and treats. Even than our behaviour was outrageous and talking amongst ourselves when we should be singing was the norm rather than the exception, not to mention the odd bouts of pushing and shoving. We had liitle regard for his authority and most of his instructions we simply ignored. I think our bad behaviour was certainly the major reason why Mr Charlesworth resigned. I now feel sad and ashamed that a decent man should have been given such a hard time.

The new choirmaster was George Senior, a relative of mine, who was young and enthusiastic. He and his wife Muriel never had any children and I'm sure they looked on us lads as a boisterous substitute family. Besides being an excellent choir trainer and organist, George had a personality, which suited us fine. He'd join in our football and cricket games on the vicarage lawn and have a joke with us, but even he had a bit of a tussle to bring us back in order.

We looked forward with eager anticipation to the highlight of the year - the choir trip, which George organised each June to a seaside resort within bus travelling distance. I don't think George would have much opposition in the Church Council when he asked for the sizeable grant to cover the cost. He'd always book lunch and high tea at one of the best hotels, which for us hungry lads was a real treat. The afternoons were usually spent playing cricket on the beach, or in the case of a visit to Scarborough a round of mini golf. On one occasion, Edward Blackburn, who was not a choir member but a sidesman who'd come along, took an almighty swing at his golf ball. It was a magnificent drive, apart from its wayward direction. It landed first bounce on the road alongside the course. There was a loud noise of glass being shattered and a large plate glass window was in ruins. Edward was indeed flustered, but I can't remember how the incident was finally resolved.

Above all however, we had great respect for George's musical ability and soon he raised the standard of the choir enormously. He taught us the tonic sol-fah system, which was a tremendous help to those who could not read music. Soon we were singing a broad range of traditional 4 part anthems every Sunday and he introduced a new pointing[2] for the Psalms. The Psalter we used was by Bishop Coverdale and first appeared in 1535. This supreme work, along with the roughly contemporary Book of Common Prayer are, in my view, one of the glories of English literature. I thoroughly enjoyed singing anthems, the ones I remember best were *The Wilderness*, *What Are These*, *Come Holy Ghost* and *Rejoice in the Lord Alway* – the latter often known as the Bell Anthem on account of its long chime-like introduction. In every facet of our singing George insisted on precision and clear diction – something of a feat for roughly spoken village lads and he was a stickler for good intonation (trebles have a tendency to sing sharp). I'm certain that the choir developed into one of the finest church choirs of its day and, at its best, probably not far short of cathedral standard.

The choir practice on Wednesday evenings was solely for the boy trebles and after the first half hour of the Friday practice we were joined by the men. There were usually between 12 and 16 boy trebles, but this varied from time to time as boys left when their voices broke and new ones joined the ranks. There was approximately the same number of men divided between alto, tenor and bass lines. The choir was fortunate in having an excellent alto section including Eddie Wray (incidentally also a talented dance band pianist with The Skyliners[3]), Harold Batty and Dennis Tipler.

Eventually, I rose through the ranks to become head boy on the Decani[4] side, whilst friend Garth occupied the same position on the Cantoris side. Fortunately, Garth had a better voice than I had so he usually took the burden of the treble solos and I was thus often spared that agony. Christmas carol services could be a trial since there were often several treble solos usually shared between Garth, myself and other senior boys. Solos for the men could also test their nerve and we, as boys, always waited eagerly for Ben Dickinson, a stalwart tenor, to render 'deaths dread sting' (quite a tongue twister) as 'deaths dead string'. He managed this feat on every occasion and it was for us a source of huge hilarity and a fair amount sniggering.

In terms of our behaviour, George had certainly curtailed many of the in-church misdemeanours. However, there was still a problem with boys talking during the sermon. The vicar, Mr Legg, often stopped mid-sentence and looked down sternly from the pulpit with his disapproving eye at his recalcitrant trebles. This was usually enough to quieten us but on some occasions the

St Augustine's, Scissett Boy Choristers, 1948

*Boys from the left: G. Hutchinson, Myself, C. Wilkinson, K. Turner, P. Tatchell, P. Brook
A. Merritt, J. Hallas, G. Beamont, G. Fisher (Partly Hidden)
M. Lodge, D. Exley, J. Booth
Behind standing: G. Senior (Organist & Choirmaster) Front (Seated): W.H. Legg (Vicar)*

choir men sitting in the stalls behind us were not averse to administering a sharp clip on the ear.

After we had been let out from choir practice on dark evenings the inhabitants of the stone terrace houses in Water Street, Fleet Street, Saville Street and Dearne Street had a horrid time. Whilst our behaviour left much to be desired, we never deliberately caused damage to property or intimidated people. Knocking on doors and simply running away was pretty tame stuff so we livened things up by roping together (with clothes line) adjacent doors in the row and knocking on both simultaneously. A little bit of slack in the rope ensured that a noisy tug of war ensued. Another favourite, though somewhat mean trick, was to lean a brush against the door with a tin can of water, taken from the mucky River Dearne, on top. The houses didn't have porches so, on the door being opened, the deluge went straight into the living room.

We picked our targets carefully choosing those who would rise to the bait, and we never bothered the elderly people. Raymond Ellery, who lived in the top house in Water Street could always be relied upon to give chase. On one occasion, however, he was ready for us. I reckon that we hadn't rapped more than once on his door and he was after us like a greyhound out of a trap. I tore across the ruins intending to hide in some bushes but he was too quick for me and he gave my ears a good boxing, which I thoroughly deserved. Of course, we never told our parents about such incidents since they would have been totally unsympathetic, believing that we received what our bad behaviour merited.

Another of our tricks, although we didn't do this too often, was to cover the organ air intake grill with a raincoat when George was playing. The lack of air caused the pitch of the notes to flatten dramatically akin to the sound of a dying cow. Naturally, George was very unhappy with this antic, particularly on the occasion when prolonged covering caused the electric motor to burn out. Another occasional trick we used to play on George involved his nearly new car, an Austin 10. We would hide in the bushes behind his parked car, and when he attempted to drive away we would rush out and grab hold of the rear bumper. He'd rev the engine even harder, slip the clutch and eventually he'd overcome our combined strength. These, and all our other minor tricks, such as hiding his large print copy of Hymns A&M, he took in good part. As boys, we loved George's sense of fun and together with his superb musicianship we really did hold him in high regard. Not only that, we had a genuine affection for him.

The choir was, of course, an entirely male affair and what's more the vicar, Mr Legg was a bachelor. One could quite easily imagine that there could well have been some whiff of scandal. I can honestly say, that as far as I'm aware, no unsavoury incidents ever took place and I'm certain that if there had been, then news would have spread like wildfire amongst the boys. Surprising as it may seem, we never encountered the word homosexual until we were well in our teens – perhaps we didn't read the right newspapers!

There were, of course, other aspects of church life, although these, to a large extent, took second place to our choir commitment. The latter, although most enjoyable, was demanding. In addition to 2 rehearsals per week we sang 2 services each Sunday, Matins and Evensong. In many ways this was similar to performing 2 concerts on a weekly basis and, although set in a religious context, it's surprising how little religious fervour seemed to rub off on us. Yes, as choirboys we were all confirmed, but I think this was because it was expected of us rather than any deep religious commitment on our part at that time.

Singing in the choir took us completely out of Sunday School, although we did join in the Sunday School treats, which were always held at Bagden Hall. Similarly, we attended the Sunday School tea held in the Parish Room, usually in November. The highlight of the event came in the evening when there was a film show of old black and white comedy films organised by the Sunday School Superintendent, Willie Shaw. This may seem pretty innocent stuff and naïve by today's standards, but of course this was in the days before television.

12
LEARN OR LEAVE

Learn Or Leave – where else but in Yorkshire could you find such a forthright school motto? Even the Latin original, *Disce Aut Discede,* sounds menacing. Despite its foundation in 1392, making it the sixth oldest school in Britain, Penistone Grammar School, often simply shortened to PGS, was no public school but a traditional no-nonsense grammar school.

If my introduction to the British education system some 6 years earlier had been inauspicious then my introduction to secondary education was nothing short of a complete disaster. Even after 60 years, I can still feel my stomach churning like mad knowing that I was going to be horribly late for my first day in the new school. It wasn't simply any school day, but it was the day when each new intake of pupils sat the grading exam, the results of which determined the form they were to enter. I knew that the No. 36 Yorkshire Traction service bus to Barnsley via Denby Dale left Scissett at 8.10am and accordingly I gave myself 5 minutes to spare. I was walking briskly up the short rise to the bus stop at the post office when a red double decker flashed passed my road end in the direction of Denby Dale. I was horror struck. How on earth could I have missed the bus on such an important day? What was I to do now?

My first thought was to run the 1 1/2 miles to Denby Dale and hope that I was in time to catch my connection, the No. 33A bus to Penistone. A moment's reflection and I realised the hopelessness of that undertaking. Instead, I ran back home in a terribly confused state only to find the house door locked. I guessed immediately that Mum had probably popped down to Rock Villa to see grandma Bedford. Another 10 minutes elapsed by the time I'd returned home with Mum. In those days hardly anyone locally had a car so there was no hope of getting a lift. There was only one solution; it had to be the bike. I pedalled off up Wheatley Hill and had just passed under the railway bridge at Lower Denby, some 3 miles into my journey, when mechanical disaster struck. The clip holding the rear mudguard fractured allowing the mudguard to rub along the tyre. I knocked on a cottage door and a friendly lady gave me some string and I was able to effect a temporary repair. All this was losing me time. I knew that the No. 33A bus to Penistone, the one I was supposed to have caught in Denby Dale, had not overtaken me, so I assumed (correctly) that it was already ahead of me and had probably reached my destination by now. Furiously I pedalled the last 4 miles and arrived at the school in a tremendous sweat, and flustered too!

I had no idea how late I was since I didn't have a watch. I'd never been to the school before, so I simply walked through the first door I saw – later I found out that this was the girls' entrance. The school was eerily silent, only the grading exam was taking place. The corridor was deserted and I crept along it quietly and eventually found the assembly hall on my left. I peered through the glass window in the door and saw the new entrants sitting at rows of desks, heads down, writing intently. Terrified and still panting slightly, I summoned up enough courage to push open the door and was met by a stern faced man. I didn't know it at the time but this was the senior master, Mr Robinson, known to generations of Penistonians as Froggy – yes, he taught French! I whispered my name and a brief explanation. For the only time ever, I saw Froggy smile as he put his hand on my shoulder and propelled me to a vacant desk at the back of the hall. I can't remember too much about the exam except that we had a Maths paper and an English paper. We were then free to return home before lunch.

How is it I missed the bus to school? Well, in actual fact I didn't – I only thought I had. What neither Mum nor I knew at the time was that there were two Yorkshire Traction buses leaving Scissett within 5 minutes of each other. The first one had brought workers to Beanland's Mill and the second one was the normal

No.36 service bus. It was the earlier mill bus, which I had seen departing and wrongly assumed that this was the service bus. After such a traumatic experience, I made jolly sure I never missed the bus again during the whole of my PGS career.

Penistone Grammar School Form IIIA, Summer Term 1949
Back row from left: P. Skeldon, J.L Halstead, S. Chappell A.I Ward, P. Sanderson, Myself, Robert Hill, G. Swift, R. Stirk, B. Blackburn
Middle row from left: A. Fieldsend, J. Curry, D. Freeman, J. Hoyland, R. Nicholson, D. Jackson, B. Auckland, C. Jubb, Rodney Hill, M. Birkenshaw, G. Belcher, E. Pearce, R.Senior, F. Taylor, B. Nichols, K. Dearnley, S. Tomlinson, P. Adams, V. Whittle.
Front row from left:A. Branston, A. Allsop, P. Lockwood, Mr J. Nelson(Form Master), B. Moorhouse, M. Helliwell, B. Sykes

By my second day at PGS, with the whole school now assembled, was a huge disappointment and in many ways was a threatening and daunting experience. The disappointment centred entirely on being assigned to Form IIB rather than the academically superior Form IIA. Looking back on it, given the handicap I suffered in the grading exam the previous day, I was actually pretty lucky not to end up in Form IIC. Incidentally, the school had a curious tradition of Year One Forms being designated II rather than the logical I, the reason for which I never discovered.

For the first few weeks in my new school I suffered a thoroughly miserable time and I would have given anything to escape. By modern standards the school was quite small. With a 3 Form entry each year and about 35 in each form, the entire school population, including a VIth form of about 50, was around the 350 mark. For a youngster of 11, who had come from a small village school, the sheer numbers seemed overwhelming. The most frightening aspect was the 'fagging system' in which older boys bullied the newcomers and had them carrying out the most demeaning tasks. Any weakness in the new starters was exploited and ridicule was a common feature of new school life. In my case, my blond wavy hair was parted on the right (traditionally the girls side) and I was teased and made fun of unmercifully.

Such treatment isn't harmful physically, but it can be a psychological torture. I felt lonely, insecure and totally isolated since I knew only one boy in school, Peter Hutchinson. He was 6 years older and therefore I had little contact with him. I knew only one girl, Audrey Calvert, who was a contemporary and had passed the 11 Plus exam with me at Scissett – but then, in this new regime, boys and girls didn't have much contact either. Most of the new starters were in the fortunate position of being amongst contemporaries from the same junior school, which often had supplied up to a dozen or so entrants each. The morning break and lunch times were, for me, sheer hell and I would do anything to avoid going out amongst the seething mass. Often I would hang about in my Form Room (Room 1 as it was then) until everyone had gone and then I would hide myself behind the massive in-line aero engine of pre-war vintage in the corner of the room. I can remember Mr Cartwright, the school caretaker, discovering me on only one occasion. Incidentally, I never found out why the school should have this antique piece of engineering, nor indeed the airframe, which occupied the Netherfields end of the playing fields.

The misery I suffered was unrelenting and each weekend came as sheer relief, although of course, as Sunday evenings wore on, I became extremely anxious once more. Despite being desperately unhappy, I somehow managed to make it through to the half term holiday and on returning after the break things suddenly seemed to become easier. The older boys no longer bullied quite as hard and by this time I'd managed to join in one or two groups at break time and dinner time (in Yorkshire, lunch was always called dinner). The second half of the first term was by no means as stressful and I actually began to enjoy some aspects of the new challenging environment.

It soon became apparent that *Learn or Leave* was something more than a motto and from time to time this was applied to some unfortunate recalcitrant. School discipline was strictly enforced and the majority of teachers certainly would not tolerate any fooling around in class. I didn't find the academic study too difficult, although it was intensive and quite a step up from the more leisurely pace of junior school. The formal approach to lessons suited me fine. I was delighted to begin a serious study of the sciences, as I'd always been very interested in such matters from an early age, having read the appropriate sections of several encyclopaedias.

Physics and chemistry were my absolute forte. My knowledge and ability in these subjects was soon recognised amongst my classmates who gave me the nickname 'molecule'. Without too much effort on my part, I usually came top or near top in these subjects through to the fifth form. I was less enthused with biology - topics such as the digestive system of the frog hardly set me alight! Mathematics was split into 3 subjects algebra, arithmetic and geometry. At first, I found algebra something of a puzzle until I'd figured out the concept of minus numbers and how to handle them.

French was the foreign language everyone learnt in the first year and I realised fairly early on that I wasn't going to make a brilliant linguist – I simply couldn't bear the drudgery of committing to memory the huge word lists we were expected to learn for homework each week. The study of English was divided into 2 main branches, English Language and English Literature. Language covered the basic grammatical elements such as punctuation, spelling and sentence analysis. Although it seemed a bore (and at times, something of a mystery too), analysis stood me in good stead in later life when I came to study German, in which grammatical correctness is fundamental. Even today I can still remember such complications as subject and predicate, noun clause objects and such like phrases of mystery, which would today flummox most 11 year olds.

Other first year subjects were history, geography and RE, all of which I thoroughly enjoyed and in which I could coast along in relative comfort. The school engendered a competitive ethos and form positions were all important. At the end of the first term all the new entrants sat the same examination and a mass re-grading exercise was based on the results. After the Christmas holiday, along with around half a dozen others, I was delighted to be moved up to the A Form, where I remained to the end of GCE 'O' level.

First and foremost, the school prided itself on its academic prowess, but looking back it is now apparent that the majority of the teaching effort was concentrated on the A form, with the B and C forms proceeding at a slower pace. Such was the pressure on the A form, that from the end of the first academic year onwards, there was no realistic possibility of a pupil from a lower form being promoted. The reason was a simple one. The school, having selected its 'star' pupils into the A form by the end of the first year, then worked them at a very fast pace in order that they could complete the GCE 'O' level course after only 4 years of study. In contrast, the B and C forms worked at a slower pace, which prepared them for the examination at the end of 5 years, the time scale envisaged by the Ministry of Education.

Despite promotion being effectively denied to the B and C form pupils after the first year, the threat of demotion weighed heavily on us in the A form. The criterion for demotion appeared to be simply the form position based on examination results. The calculation of form position was by no means transparent and seemed to be something of a black art, certainly as far as the pupils were concerned. I rather suspect that mathematics and English received a higher weighting than other subjects to reflect the greater time spent on these subjects. There were about 34 pupils in my A form, a figure which seemed to stay pretty static through to the end of Form VA. Anyone lower than about 30th felt vulnerable. Although I was less than middling in English[1] and foreign languages[2], my results in maths, the sciences, along with history and geography ensured that I was always positioned somewhere between 8th and 12th, a safe zone by a considerable margin.

There were some exceptionally bright sparks in my form. This is not surprising considering the huge size of the catchment area. In a north-south direction this stretched from the boundary of Huddersfield in the north to the Sheffield boundary in the south, a distance of almost 20 miles. The eastern boundary was Barnsley and the western included Holmfirth, a distance of around 12 miles. I don't know what proportion of children from the catchment area attended PGS, but it was probably quite small. The two unchallenged stars of my form were Bob Senior from Stocksbridge and Doris Jackson from Oxspring, who were always vying for top spot. They were both naturally gifted and neither seemed to work tremendously hard to achieve their success. Frances Taylor too was always a front runner.

In my view, the school was, in the main, blessed with excellent and committed teachers. From my own point of view, two young teachers who arrived whilst I was studying for 'O' levels were nothing less than outstanding. Sheila Stead had taught geography in the Northeast and brought tremendous enthusiasm to her subject – even to the extent of using the very latest visual aids of the day, filmstrips and the epidiascope[3], to illustrate her lessons. Sheila remained at Penistone for the remainder of her career and became Senior Mistress and Deputy Head. John O'Connell, known to us as Jock, was Irish and came to teach us history. He brought a refreshing approach to the subject, teaching not only the facts but also exploring the reasons and causes of historical events. Jock moved on to become head of the history department at what became Huddersfield University. These two teachers fired my enthusiasm for their subjects, the continued study and enjoyment of which has enhanced my life.

The 1944 Education Act, designed to afford equal educational opportunity based on academic merit, had certainly worked in our case. Apart from three whose parents were teachers and two from modest shop owning families, the rest of us were truly working class. Despite the academic pressure, which the school placed on us, as a group we gelled together extremely well[4]. There was certainly no unpleasant rivalry and, as far as I can recall, no cliques developed. We had plenty of fun and laughs together and often groups would meet up at weekends and during school holidays to follow a particular bent or activity. In summer, a day out in the sun at Bramall Lane, Sheffield to watch Yorkshire compete in the County Championship was popular with the boys.

Fundamental to the learning process was the strict discipline enforced from the moment we set foot inside the school until we left at the end of the day. The morning assembly was run on military lines. Each form marched into the hall starting with the junior forms, the girls entering through the front door and the boys through the rear. In the hall, every form was put into line by school prefects with military precision with the lower forms at the front. A narrow aisle separated the girls on the right side of the hall from the boys on the left. The senior master, 'Froggy', stood on the stage to oversee this drill. He had a fearsome reputation and had only to whip his glasses off and stare menacingly to guarantee absolute silence. Of course, we were not supposed to speak, even in whispers, during the wait for the headmaster, Mr Bowman, to make his grand entrance. He was an imposing figure, who the pupils always referred to as 'The Boss'. This description seems to me entirely appropriate, for he, along with Froggy and to a lesser extent Mrs Gathercole, the senior mistress, ruled the empire with a rod of iron. The Boss imposed his will almost entirely through his strong, stern personality, although he was not averse to using the cane on a determined recalcitrant and he had, as a final resort, expulsion as the ultimate deterrent.

The military ethos extended into the classroom where boys and girls were again segregated, but this time the boys were on the right and the girls on the left. In the classrooms we were always seated in single desks in rows stretching back from the front. Before a teacher entered the room it was expected that we should already be sitting down in surname alphabetical order commencing at the front. To this day I can still remember the boys alphabetical list: Auckland, Belcher, Blackburn, Chappell, Freeman, Halstead, Hellewell and so on. My alphabetical position ensured I always ended up in the back corner – a handy position when questions were being asked around the class. Incidentally, the boys were always addressed by their surnames and the girls by their Christian names. Each school year we had a different form room where daily registration took place and all our books not wanted for homework could be left in our assigned desks. To be able to leave our books was a great advantage saving us the burden of lugging everything home in our leather satchels. Despite our desks being unsecured, it was entirely safe to leave personal belongings – woe betides any pupil found prying into someone else's desk!

In addition to the strict academic rigour, the school laid great store on sport and games and the result of every school match, which had been played on the Saturday morning, was ritually announced in the Monday morning assembly. Penistone's climate, as a result of its situation high in the foothills of the

Pennine moors wasn't the most conducive to enjoyment of outside games and sport. It was always reckoned that Penistone railway station was the coldest in England and I can testify from personal experience to the bitterly cold winter winds sweeping across the school playing fields. The boys, during the autumn and winter terms, were subjected to 3 sessions of Physical Education (PE). The indoor activity was in the gym, which at least had the advantage of avoiding the usually dreadful weather. I didn't like gym work since we seemed to be standing around an awful lot waiting our turn to fling ourselves over the box or the horse. This activity carried a grave risk of a fall or a bad landing resulting in some pain at least and a broken ankle or wrist at worst. I never saw the point of hanging aimlessly from the wall bars and the floor exercises didn't seem to achieve much either. The gym sessions I would rate as useless for developing either muscular strength or flexibility and achieved absolutely nothing towards cardio-vascular system improvement.

In contrast, our weekly cross-country run (always known as 'a cross') certainly tested and improved the heart and lung function. There were a series of graded courses, mostly heading off in the Thurlstone direction, although at one stage the Penistone bypass was used as part of the courses. The shortest run was about 3 miles for the junior boys moving up to one of about four and a half miles for the middle boys and finally the senior boys were expected to tackle a 6 mile course. The turning point for the senior course was at High Bank on the moors high above Thurlstone and I can remember my lungs nearly bursting and my legs aching and almost feeling like jelly. On many occasions, a biting wind was driving the snow almost horizontally, which stung our faces and legs. Despite the arctic conditions we were sweating profusely. Being clothed in nothing more than a sports vest and shorts and without modern hi-tech road running shoes (we just wore canvas 'pumps'), it's a wonder that a serious incident never occurred. To give a flavour of these events and to show I'm not exaggerating, the following is an extract from a school magazine report of the 1951 senior race in which I participated:

171

*Throughout the morning, the stalwarts kept glancing apprehensively out of tightly closed windows wondering whether they would have to venture into 'polar' conditions, clad in outfits, which even in summer are thought by some to be scanty, but for a gale in mid-winter quite insufficient! As the keen 'northeaster' prevailed with excessive quantities of snow until dinner time, general opinion was in favour of a postponement, as exposure seemed suicidal, for to cover the distance to the canteen required much skill and nerve. At 2.30 the bell went and runners went to their various changing rooms to emerge a few moments later and walk ditheringly to the bottom of Long Lane; then after the last farewells a mad stampede was in progress. This consisted not only of cross-country runners, but also a herd of terrified cattle, which the moment before had been ambling contentedly along, but now, to the farmer's amazement, suddenly reversed at the sight of a road full of humans charging amid a cloud of ice and snow. This incident caused the state of the weather to be forgotten temporarily, as the procession scrambled its way along Red Ridge to the snowdrifts of High Bank. Would tomorrow's headlines be "**50 PGS Students Perished in Blizzard**?" The run back down coated everyone with a half- inch layer of snow and but for the fact that we were more or less mobile, we should be on the hill-tops in cold storage. After crossing the fields, where skis would have been more suitable than running shoes, and stiles where our legs turned to jelly, we ran, or rather staggered, into the final stretch.*

Today, I'm sure boys, rightly, would never be sent out in such atrocious conditions.

Football (soccer) for me was also a trial. I was a passable enough player, but again the conditions made it extremely unpleasant. The playing fields were exposed and the biting wind, rain and snow were certainly not to my liking. The pitch was usually muddy or frozen hard and in the former conditions the leather ball soaked up the water and it was akin to playing with a sand bag. To head such a weighty object was now suicidal. The undoubted football star of my year was Rodney Hill from Stocksbridge. Rodney played at inside forward (in the days when players occupied recognisably defined positions) and he was the automatic choice for the regional South West Yorkshire boys, whose home ground was Sheffield Wednesday's Hillsborough. I still wonder why he never turned professional - perhaps he lost his enthusiasm for the game?

The summer term usually brought better weather. Football gave way to cricket and cross country runs were replaced by field and track athletics. I was quite a decent cricketer and enjoyed batting and keeping wicket. The star of my year at cricket was Raymond Stirk from Hade Edge. Raymond, I'm sure could have made county standard with proper coaching but he, nevertheless, became an outstanding batsman with the Holmfirth and Paddock cricket clubs in the very competitive Huddersfield League. In athletics I never shone. Although I had a good cardio-vascular system my basic running speed wasn't great – perhaps this could be attributed to the fact that I rode the bicycle a lot and therefore developed the wrong leg muscles. For the throwing events, javelin, discus and shot, I simply hadn't the physical strength to compete with the best. Despite these limitations I still enjoyed myself out on the athletics field and as a bonus there was always the opportunity to watch the girls!

The highlight of the summer term was the annual inter grammar schools athletics championships held at the cricket ground at Fartown, Huddersfield. The entire school decamped there for the afternoon's events, everyone boarding buses with great excitement and anticipation immediately after an early school dinner. The boys' competition was usually a tussle between Hemsworth Grammar and Normanton Grammar with the other boys' teams trailing well behind in third and lower places. The girls' competition was a different story. In the years I attended, PGS was invincible. They simply didn't just scramble a win, but triumphed each year by a colossal margin. This wasn't surprising since the team was led by Heather Armitage, an outstanding track athlete. She was an Empire Games medallist who went on to represent Great Britain in the sprint events at the Helsinki Olympics. Incidentally, Heather set the UK record for the 100 yards in the 1950's, a mark, which stood for well over 20 years. Heather was ably supported by many fine girl athletes including Irene Morris and from my form, Audrey Branston.

House competitions were a feature of the school's sporting tradition. The school was divided into 4 houses; Armitage (yellow), Bosville (blue), Clarel (red) and Dransfield (green), the names being those of important late Medieval families of the district. I was a rather inert member of Dransfield and I now have a confession to make. In the two games in which I could have made a mark at school, that is, football and most certainly cricket, I never tried too hard to impress. I simply played at a level to avoid appearing totally useless. Quite frankly, I didn't want to be involved in playing matches outside school hours. Why? It occurred to me within weeks of starting at PGS that if I missed the special school bus home (nicknamed The Denby Dale Cronk), which travelled directly to Scissett I would have to catch a 33A service bus to Denby Dale. There, I would then be faced with a choice of either waiting 45 minutes with no bus shelter in order to catch a No. 36 connection to Scissett or walk home the mile and a half in all weathers. House matches were always played after school and it would have been late evening before I arrived home. To have been picked for one of the school teams, which invariably played their matches on Saturday mornings, would have meant considerable inconvenience in terms of travel. Furthermore, I would have had to spend most of the day away from home and I felt I'd better things to do.

The very poor travel connection between Scissett and Penistone impacted on my school life in other ways too. A Combined Cadet Force had been formed and the training involved staying behind after school for certainly one and sometimes two evenings each week. Despite the amount of 'square bashing', I certainly enjoyed my initial involvement with the Force, covering such diverse topics as map reading, field tactics, and care of the ubiquitous 303 rifle. However, the ever present travel difficulty, and with Dad firmly against any military aspirations on my part, I decided to resign. This certainly did not go down well with 'The Boss', who as an ex-military man was an enthusiastic supporter of the Cadets to the point that he often wore his army uniform in school. I was called to his study to justify my decision, not simply to explain it. He made me feel as though I was letting myself, the school and the country down. Believe me, it was an unpleasant experience. From that point in time he seemed to have little regard for me and only spoke to me as an individual once after that. He simply treated me as a non-person right through my school career. On entering the VIth form it was assumed that everyone would be appointed a monitor or prefect. When my time came, I was the only boy of my year not to be granted that distinction - I certainly felt acute disappointment and humiliation.

The sole occasion 'The Boss' spoke to me as an individual after my resignation from the Cadets came about through music. I had great regard for Harold Healey, who was the school's part-time music teacher as well as organist at Holmfirth Parish Church. Harold had catholic tastes in music and had many connections in the orchestral and brass band worlds. I often chatted to him about music and concerts I had played in or attended and I knew he'd heard me perform with the trombone – in either band concerts or contests. Harold was putting together an afternoon musical concert for the whole school with a variety of performers – choirs, vocalists and pianists. Out of the blue he asked me if I'd agree to play a solo. I chose *The Acrobat*, the performance turning out to be a 'show stopper'. Harold was delighted and backstage afterwards 'The Boss' sought me out and said something like: "well done, that must have taken some courage." At least, he belatedly acknowledged me.

Those, like myself, in form VA completed the CGE 'O' level course in 4 years and it was automatically expected by the school that we would continue into the VIth form. Perhaps I should have left and gone out to work at that stage, because my enthusiasm for the school and schoolwork was at a low ebb. However, against my better judgement, I did continue into the VIth form and studied maths, physics and chemistry at 'A' level. Of course, I'm not the first one to have experienced at first hand the significant increased academic rigour demanded by 'A' levels compared to the rather easy canter of 'O' levels. I had many external distractions and calls on my time, mainly in the brass band world. To be perfectly frank, I lacked commitment to study hard. I suppose too that I was on the arrogant side, academically speaking, and with maths, in particular, I just assumed that I was good enough to work things out from first principles. This may or may not have been true, but sitting examinations with a time constraint nothing beats learning all formulae and practising mathematical techniques through lots of worked examples, something in my case largely lacking.

By the time of the 'A' level examinations, I was champing at the bit to leave and enter the world of work. In common with all but the very progressive schools, careers guidance was but a low priority, in fact virtually non-existent. The steel works paid well, although the dust and heat produced by the flaming infernos, which were the Bessemer Converters, didn't appeal one bit. Textile mills had long hours and poor pay, but one had the advantage of working amongst, hopefully, attractive girls. Heights had never fazed me, so, through my Dad's connections, an apprenticeship with a Huddersfield firm of steeplejacks was a distinct possibility. The pay was decent enough with excellent outdoor views, but on reflection I couldn't see much merit in being stuck on top of a 100-metre high mill chimney in the Colne Valley with snow blasting horizontally off the Pennines. However, after looking at those options I decided to enter the coal mining industry with its short hours underground and excellent pay. The choice wasn't based upon long-term career opportunities, but rather upon seemingly short-term superficial attractions. As my final term in school ground on, I couldn't wait to start earning some money. My release came when I left school immediately after sitting my last 'A' level examination. That was on a Friday towards the middle of June and I reported at the pit at 7.00am the following Monday, several weeks before the school had officially broken up. Today, I bet one couldn't do that in an era now bound up with so much Health and Safety red tape!

13
IN THE BLACK

My early working life put me in the black in more ways than one. Anyone who has been underground in a coalmine will, almost certainly, have experienced total darkness. Even if the visit into the bowels of the earth has only been as a tourist, it is odds on that the guide will have encouraged everyone to switch their lights off at some stage. Then it's black, and I mean black.

It's blacker than any paint, which could be created on the surface of the earth. Underground without a light there's no shadow, no silhouette, no reflection, no perspective – absolutely nothing. It was in this black world that much of my early working life was spent. Coal is black too and underground on the coalface it's impossible to avoid thick clouds of black coal dust sticking to one's sweating body and face. On the coalface for several hours each day, my face was jet black, even my lips were caked with free black lipstick, with only the whites of my eyes to reveal to a casual visitor that I was indeed a human being. Those were just some of the downsides of being a collier, but a bank balance healthily in the black was, for me, one of the upsides. Yes, when I started work in the early 1950's, the industry hadn't been long out of private ownership and the universal cry was 'coal at any price'. The post-war years were marked by one fuel crisis after another. In this economic climate the pits were working a $5^{1}/_{2}$day week and miners were top of the first division pay league.

My introduction to this hostile environment didn't occur until some months after I'd started work at Park Mill Colliery, Clayton West. During the run-up to leaving school, I'd mentioned to a near neighbour, Tom Davidson, that I fancied going into mining. Tom was some sort of accountant with the National Coal Board (NCB). He was one of the few people in the village who always dressed smartly for work, so I assumed he must have been of some standing and he clearly had connections with people in management. Quite out of the blue, I received a message from Arthur Hinchliffe's secretary asking if I wanted an interview with her boss, mentioning that Tom had 'put a word in for me'. Mr Hinchliffe, as he was always known to the workman, was Agent for a group of 4 collieries, Park Mill, Emley Moor, Bullcliffe Wood and Denby Grange, which made up the Park Mill Sub Area of the Yorkshire Division's No.6 (North Barnsley) Area. During the interview with Mr Hinchliffe, it became apparent that he had great regard for my grandfather, John Edward Bedford. John Edward had been a mining contractor[1] who had undertaken several capital projects for the Stringer Company, who were the pre-nationalisation owners of Park Mill and Emley Moor collieries at the time that Mr Hinchliffe was employed as a young under official.

My interview went extremely well and, although it was unspoken, I gained the distinct impression that Mr Hinchliffe would take me under his wing. He noted that I'd studied science 'A' levels and remarked that this would be a good basis for a worthwhile career in the industry. However, he made it very clear that I would have to undertake further study at technical college to gain the government certificates[2], which were a legal requirement for anyone holding a post of responsibility in the industry. Furthermore, I would have to obtain several years of practical experience before I could sit the Mining Qualifications Board examinations and accordingly there would be no escape from hard manual work. To set me on the road, he promised that he would arrange for me to do a variety of work so that I could gain all-round experience in mining and not be stuck forever in one job. Park Mill colliery, the nearest pit to my home, would be my posting. He was as good as his word and soon I received a message to report to the pit office where I met, for the first time, Mr Redgewick the Colliery Manager. He was a bit on the gruff side, but clearly he was going to act on the recommendation from above and allow me a variety of work experience. How's that for luck?

It was with some trepidation that I donned old clothes and pedalled off for my first day in work. At 7.00am I reported to Bert Fisher, who was the yard foreman, and he set me to work in the supplies yard. Here I loaded tubs and trams with wooden props of varying length, lids[3], split bars[4], bricks, stemming[5], rails, girders and all manner of consumables for use underground. I'd then to push the tubs and trams out of the yard on a narrow gauge rail track, turn them manually on a 'flag' (a thick iron sheet) onto a second track to make up a 'run' prior to them being taken underground by rope haulage.

After four hours of hard manual labour I was ready for a rest and a bite of 'snap', which was taken sitting down with the other men in the open air. Mum had provided some sandwiches and a flask of tea. All too soon, the break was over and it was back to the repetitive slog. The end of the day eventually arrived and at 4.00pm I pedalled off home feeling absolutely worn out. Of course, such a prolonged spell of manual work was alien to me. By the end of my 3week stint in the supplies yard, my muscles had grown more accustomed to the new regime and I was certainly considerably stronger and fitter than when I started. Although this work may appear to be very menial and boring, which in truth it was, through it I learnt quite a bit about underground coal mining and the supplies necessary to keep such operations running.

My next job was far more technical and it allowed me to pick up some skills useful in later life. I was sent to work in the fitting shop. I reported to the Unit Engineer, George William Scargill, always referred to as George William and no relation to the future NUM president Arthur. He'd obviously been primed and through him I had the good fortune to be assigned as Doug Whittle's temporary assistant. Doug, the fitting shop foreman, although a shade abrupt at times, was a thoroughly skilled mechanical engineer and actually a very good teacher. I was given a bench overlooking the pit yard, with my own tool drawer and vice. This was alongside Doug's position and ideal for him to keep an eye on me. Dressed in a navy boiler suit and sporting a 2 foot steel rule in the long pocket on the right trouser leg, as all proper mechanics did, it wasn't long before I began to feel the part. Initially, much of my work centred round the use of hand tools, files, hacksaw, taps and dies etc and I quickly picked up the engineering terminology. For some reason, I was spared the indignity of being sent to the stores for a putty hammer or elbow grease, a joke played on most new apprentices.

Soon, I was let loose on an old fashioned lathe driven by an overhead line shaft – changing speed was a tricky operation involving a fair amount of dexterity with the leather drive belt. I tackled, reasonably successfully, a variety of plain turning jobs under guidance from Doug. Eventually he deemed me skilled enough to attempt the quite advanced turning of specific sized balls on a mandrel and also the cups to enclose these. My first efforts weren't all that successful and Doug, ever one for the colourful turn of phrase, condemned them with the remark "there's as much slack in those as a turd in a pisspot." These balls and cups formed part of the mechanism to allow a face conveyor belt to twist over – a very successful innovation for working in thin seams. I believe, although I cannot be certain, that this modification to the conveyor gear head was invented, designed and developed by George William. A wide variety of underground machinery was brought into the shop for repair or renovation and I soon became familiar with the workings of coal cutters, haulage engines, pumps, compressed air drills etc and I assisted with stripping them down and rebuilding.

The fitting shop contained not only the usual heavy machinery; lathes, boring machines, millers, shapers etc used by the 20 or so fitters and turners, but also housed the hearths of about 7 blacksmiths. In one corner there was also a small furnace used for brass and cast iron moulding employing 3 people including a pattern maker. Adjoining, was the welding shop employing 4 people. This was a place to avoid at all costs. The thick acrid fumes generated in the confined poorly ventilated space caused the eyes to smart within a couple of minutes – heaven only knows what havoc was wreaked on the lungs of those working in there

Park Mill Colliery, circa 1950
Fitting shop and attached welding shop shown to the left of the pit yard.
My workbench was behind the 2ⁿᵈ window from the left

permanently. The boss welder, whose name I've forgotten, was an evil and short tempered chap whose brain must also have been affected by the fumes. On one occasion, because of the noise, I didn't hear a remark he'd addressed to me and was rewarded with a 3lb (1.37kg) hammer striking me in the mid-riff. This he'd thrown at me from a range of about 2 metres. I didn't need to retaliate, for the others who'd witnessed the unsavoury incident downed tools immediately and jumped to my defence directing a stream of invective at him causing him to slink off in shame.

My time spent in the fitting shop gave me an insight into a wide range of engineering and allied skills, even though I didn't practice them all myself, as well as affording me a good working knowledge of mining machinery. The highlight of my week was Friday, for, in addition this being payday[6], the youngest apprentice[7] was detailed off to fetch the 'snap time' fish and chips from Hardcastle's 'chip shop' situated up nearby Scott Hill.

Park Mill pit had a long history dating well back into the nineteenth century and because it was situated pretty much on the outcrop of the New Hards and Wheatley Lime coal seams, its focus had migrated several times. Consequently, there were no fewer than 6 entrances to the underground workings – 2 vertical shafts and 4 drifts[8]. The main surface installations of the colliery, which included the fitting shop and supplies yard, were situated on a site several acres in extent adjacent to the main A636 road just behind the Junction Inn at Park Mill. Also on this site were the main offices, the electric shop, the carpenters' shop, the stores and just to the north was the huge spoil heap, always known as the 'muckstack'. This site also contained the mouth of a drift at a gradient of 1 in 6.38 heading off under Hagg Hill, which was used to transport supplies into the mine by means of a rope haulage. There was also an old vertical shaft, depth only about 60 yards (55m), which was used as a pumping shaft.

One advantage of working in the fitting shop and being Doug's gofer was the opportunity it afforded for visiting other surface installations of the colliery, which were scattered around the locality. Shortly after nationalisation and a couple or so years before I started work, it had undergone a substantial reconstruction, which cost £300,000 – a tidy sum then. A new horizon[9] mine (tunnel), 1652 yards (1510m) long, for diesel haulage and running approximately southwest from the centre of the take[10] had been driven to intersect 2 drifts to the surface, one at a gradient of 1 in 3.76 and one at a gradient of 1 in 12. The steeper of the two drifts, known as the Conveyor Drift, was 300 yards (274m) long and housed the main coal conveyor to the screens, which were situated adjacent to Clayton West rail terminus and approximately $^3/_4$ mile south of the main Park Mill site. The other drift, known as the Loco Drift, 700 yards (640m) long, was deliberately driven at a shallow gradient to allow the diesel locomotives to be brought out to their surface garage and also to provide a second entrance for supplies to be taken below ground by a rope haulage. The mouth of the Loco Drift and the locomotive garage were also at Park Mill, but on the opposite side of the A636 to the main surface installations.

A second vertical shaft, the Springwood Shaft, used solely for man riding, was situated in a small copse, adjacent to the A636 and some $^3/_4$ mile east of the main Park Mill site. The vast majority of underground workers used this shaft to gain access to the workings. This shaft also served as the pit's upcast ventilation shaft and was therefore equipped with an exhausting centrifugal fan at the surface. Also on this site were the lamp room, the powder magazine for explosives storage and the offices for the underground officials.

My first experience below ground was rather unusual and certainly illegal, as I had not yet undertaken the preliminary underground training required by the Coal Mines Act 1911. On the Park Mill site was an old disused drift, known, due to its limited headroom (about 1.5m) as the Low Hole (pronounced Low Oil) heading north under the muckstack. An electrically operated centrifugal pump was about 200m down the drift at the edge of flooded workings. A 6inch (15cm) pipe range ran up the drift from the pump to the surface. The pump was operated on an occasional basis and its purpose was to prevent ingress of water into the current workings. Just outbye[11] of the pump, there had been a roof collapse, which required immediate repair. The width of the drift was somewhat narrower than the main gates[12] of the current working faces and consequently the standard length straight steel support girders had to be cut to length. This was deemed to be an ideal job for me and so I was teamed up with Arthur Mountain from Emley, an experienced underground repairer to undertake the repair task.

The drift was furnished with a set of rails and, at the surface, a hand winch, which allowed us to pull up one tub of fallen rock at a time – an arm breaking task! We also used the winch to lower down the girders and props for the repair. Despite the fact that I never lost sight of daylight, this first underground experience gave me an insight into the lethal hazards inherent in mining. Fortunately, Arthur was a steady, careful worker, who during the setting of the new wooden props and steel girders, kept me well out of danger posed by any further rock fall. For me, it was a most enjoyable week's work, away from of the hurly-burly of the fitting shop.

It was during my time in the fitting shop that I learnt the results of my 'A' Level exams. In those days there wasn't the ritual and hoo-ha verging on hysteria, which the media, TV in particular, now make of this annual event. In a month notoriously quiet for news, examination results now take on the importance of a nuclear attack. Back then, one didn't even go to the school to collect the results. They were simply published in the local newspaper, in my case the Barnsley Chronicle, for the whole world to see. Although I was a shade disappointed to have failed maths, on reflection, it was hardly surprising considering the meagre amount of work I'd put in and my somewhat cavalier approach to the subject.

Luckily, the NCB had, what was certainly the most enlightened attitude of any employer regarding education and advancement. Its Ladder Plan, enabled the lowliest worker to gain qualification through study and thus promotion to the highest managerial level. This model scheme was later copied by many other industrial and commercial organisations. Accordingly, I was enrolled at Barnsley Mining and Technical College to study for the HNC in mining. The NCB scheme allowed me one day per week paid release, with the obligation to remain at college that same evening to attend the class run as part of the course. As far as my maths 'A' level was concerned, I found out from school that I'd only missed a pass by 5% and this cheered me up no end (an actual mark, rounded to the nearest 5% preceded the introduction of grades). I figured out that if I could get so near with negligible commitment, then with a modicum of effort I should be able to reach a decent standard and it would be a shame not to at least try. This decision really did add substantially to my study workload for, on my own initiative and paying my own fees, I attended two further evenings per week at Tech - pure maths one evening and applied maths the other. In taking on this heavy commitment I'd been encouraged by my colleagues in the brass band. However, it soon became apparent that the burden of one day and 3 evenings a week study, together with mandatory homework, was simply too much to allow me to continue playing regularly in a contesting band requiring 2 and sometimes 3 practices a week. I was sad to bid farewell to my band colleagues, but I know they understood.

Despite my eagerness to work underground, in many ways I was sorry to leave the fitting shop. The men had readily accepted me and were willing to share their knowledge and experience. I realised too that these were bright men who had never had a chance educationally – most had not benefited from the 1944 Education Act and therefore had been condemned to leaving school at age 14. However, after some months in the fitting shop, my mechanical engineering career came to an end when I received a visit from Stanley Whitaker, the pit's Safety and Training Officer. I was to report the following Monday to the Training Centre at Woolley Colliery to undertake my preliminary underground training.

I'll never forget my first descent into the pit. The vertical shaft at Woolley was 328 yards[13] (299m) deep – not huge compared with the shafts of the South Yorkshire Pits, which approached 1000 yards (914m), but substantially deeper than Park Mill. With some excitement I stepped into the cage along with about 10 fellow trainees and 3 instructors. The gates clanked closed and the signal bell sounded. Quite literally, the floor dropped away and I left my stomach behind. My ears began to 'pop' as the air pressure increased during the descent. I remember too the 'whoosh' as we passed the ascending cage. I realised that the journey was about to end when I suddenly felt my knees buckling as the cage decelerated rapidly. The cage came to rest with only the tinniest of bumps, testament to the skill of the winding engineman. We stumbled out into the whitewashed, brightly lit and surprisingly spacious pit bottom, where men and boys were man-handling full coal tubs in readiness for winding to the surface. It was only later that we realised our initiation ride had been something special. The winding engineman had been 'tipped the wink' that he had a cage full of trainees and so, as was customary practice, he gave us the thrill of our lives with a breath-taking drop.

My first descent in the Springwood Shaft back at Park Mill colliery was a tame affair compared to my first ride at Woolley. The shaft, only some 80 yards (73m) deep, was used solely for man riding and the speed of the cage so slow that it was almost possible to count the bricks of the shaft lining as we passed by. I'd been issued with an electric cap lamp at the lamp room window and I wore my almost pristine black hard hat (actually made of compressed cardboard), which marked me out as a new starter. My pit clothes were simply old cast-offs that were no longer fit for everyday wear. I had brown corduroy trousers with a thick leather belt on which to hang my lamp battery, a flannel shirt and an old sports jacket. The majority of pit workers then, both on the surface and underground, wore clogs and so I simply continued to wear those I'd bought several months earlier at Arthur Barber's cobblers shop. Clogs[14] were ideal since they would last almost for ever and were low maintenance too, requiring only the occasional set of new clog irons and clog nails – my first DIY job!

Feeling the part, I tagged on to a group of men in the lamp room and after the descent simply followed them the short distance from the pit bottom to the underground office[15], where I reported to the Undermanager, George Arthur Dawson and the dayshift Overman, Bob Holden. Since I'd never worked below ground before, other than during my preliminary underground training at Woolley, the Training Regulations of the Coal Mines Act 1911 stipulated that I should, for the first 20 working days, be employed under the close personal supervision of a supervising workman. This task was allotted to a chap, Ronnie Ives, who was in charge of taking supplies along the Wheatley Main roadway and down to the faces running off the No.2 East Bord roadway. I was in effect transporting and unloading similar supplies to the ones, which several months earlier, I had loaded during my first three weeks in work.

I had now joined the band of 'datlers', that is, underground men who were paid a daily rate and not on piecework. This group was a curious mixture of fit strong lads waiting their turn to train for coalface work and older men, many with broken health, who had come off the face simply because they could no longer tolerate that arduous physical work. On returning to the surface at the end of my first underground shift, I was issued with my lamp tag. This was a brass disk with an engraved number and, to this day, I can still remember it was No. 363. Men always went home with these looped, for safe keeping, on a piece of string through the jacket collar buttonhole – remember, this was in the days before Park Mill had the luxury of pit head baths! At the start of each shift the men handed in their lamp tags to obtain a lamp and the tags were the placed on numbered hooks as a method of determining, at a glance, the identities of the men currently underground. For a $7^1/_2$ hour underground shift, compared to a 9 hour surface shift, my pay had risen by some 30%[16] no wonder the pits were attractive to a young lad like me!

Completion of my 20 days under close personal supervision allowed me to be assigned a wide variety of jobs and I therefore had the opportunity to experience the full extent of underground workings which, at that time, were pretty well scattered. The reserves in the 21 inch (0.53m) thick, excellent quality New Hards seam, which had been the lifeblood of the colliery from its inception, were almost exhausted and these North faces, accessed via drifts from the No.1 East Bord roadway in the Wheatley Lime seam, had almost reached the boundary. Several times I was assigned the task of being a 'button man' at the conveyor transfer points from these faces. This could be quite a lonely job since hardly anyone passed by and it was certainly the most boring job in the universe. The only requirement was to sit down all shift and watch the coal tumbling down the chute onto the outbye conveyor, the sole physical activity was to push the stop/start button occasionally in response to the outbye conveyor stopping and starting. Nevertheless, such an existence could have its recompense for I was able to do some productive thinking about the problems and assignments of my Tech homework.

One job, which I thoroughly enjoyed was assisting Peter Graham[17], whose task was to supply the North and East faces, which were accessed by the No1. East Bord. Our first job in the morning was to collect the empty tubs and trams from the ends of the main gates, couple them into a set of about two dozen vehicles and take them up to the surface via the 1 in 6.38 gradient drift which surfaced alongside Hagg Hill. The Transport Rules strictly prohibited riding, but of course, the temptation was just too strong. On one occasion this practice landed us in a spot of bother. We were sitting on the side of the first tub, chatting and gazing at the roof to ensure we didn't bang our heads on a low roof support girder. Suddenly we were flung off as the tub crunched into a pile of debris from an overnight roof fall. Quickly we gathered our wits, grabbed the bell wires and frantically signalled Billy Hawke, the haulage engineman, to stop. He was probably dozing, for some 10 or so vehicles had been de-railed before we got a response. It then took us the best part of 2 hours to clear the fall and lever the vehicles back onto the track.

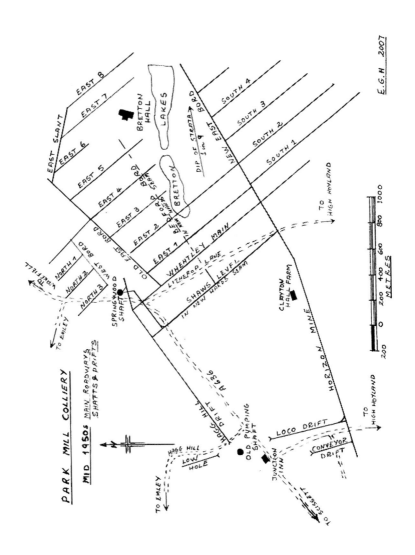

PARK MILL COLLIERY

MID 1950s MAIN ROADWAYS, SHAFTS & DRIFTS

E.G.H. 2007

Usually, if everything had gone without mishap, we were out in daylight by 'snap time' (11.00am) and if this was a Friday, then fish and chips were on the menu. After 'snap' we then picked up the full set of tubs, trams and bogeys and accompanied them underground. It was a comfortable, unhurried job with the bonus of spending an hour or so in daylight – all paid at underground rate!

A few months after I'd been working underground, the New Hards seam faces reached the boundary. I was then attached to the team of underground mechanics, led by George Fisher, salvaging coal cutters, conveyors and other machinery from those districts. This was hard physical work, often in cramped conditions, where the use of pinch bars, sylvesters[18] and lifting tackle never entirely eliminated the need for sheer brute force. In these dark and damp conditions, the potential for trapped limbs and other such extremely painful injuries was high. The dismantled pieces of machinery, often weighing in excess of a tonne, were loaded onto flat bogies and transported via the Wheatley Main roadway (a total distance of some 3km) to equip the South faces in the newly opened No. 2 East Bord[19]. Workings were now entirely in the 28 inch (0.71m) thick Wheatley Lime seam, although the East faces in that seam, accessed by the No1. East Bord, were to close shortly.

When the East faces closed, the men initially had to walk from the Springwood Shaft to their working places in the No. 2 East Bord, in some cases a distance of 2km. My next job was in connection with the upgrading of a roadway for the new diesel locomotive manrider, known as a 'paddy' to eliminate this walk. There was an existing roadway in the New Hards Seam known as Shaw's Level, but because of its small dimensions and poor condition, considerable work was required before it could be used for a heavy locomotive and train of man riding carriages. The re-construction team was headed by two very experienced stone driveage men, Walter Lodge, from Scissett and Bill Iredale from Denby Dale. Both men had each worked for about 30 years in mining and Bill's experience had also extended to excavating huge caverns for an underground hospital on the Rock of Gibraltar during his service with the Royal Engineers in World War II. In addition to Walter and Bill, who were the brains of the outfit, there were usually 2 younger lads and myself, who were there to provide the brawn.

The job was essentially to increase both the width and height of the existing roadway and to furnish it with a heavy gauge rail track. This job gave me my first real taste of mining, although not on the coalface. The team's first task at the start of the shift was to drill 2m long shot holes into the exposed roof and side – we had the luxury of compressed air drills supported on telescopic 'airlegs', this latter new innovation taking out much of the hard labour of supporting the drill on one's shoulder. Explosives were then used to blast down the roof and side leaving a huge and daunting looking muck pile. This debris had to be shovelled by hand into minecars – a difficult task since muck had to be thrown upwards to clear the top of the mine car sides, which were about 2m off the floor. Some time later during the contract, we took delivery of a Joy Loader[20], which eliminated much of the manual muck shifting. Often the blasted material contained huge lumps of rock, which were too heavy to manhandle individually and so these had to be broken up with a 7lb (3.2kg) sledge hammer. This was hard graft too and on the odd occasion a sharp flint flew into my eye, which necessitated a visit to the medical room at the end of the shift[21]. It's amazing that no serious lasting damage occurred since protective goggles weren't provided. In fact, the only protection was a pair of kneepads, which we paid for out of our wages. The newly exposed roof was supported by straight girders and these had to be lifted manually up to a height of about 4m. Sometimes we were able to stand on top of the muck pile, at other times we stood on planks on top of the mine car – either way it was a very hard lift until the girders were secured. The easier part of the job was laying the solid wooden sleepers and heavy gauge rails for the diesel locomotive track and then ballasting the track.

My first week's wage on this new job brought a huge surprise and a pleasant one too. I was now a contractor on piecework earning up to about £10 a week – double my day wage earnings! Walter and Bill were probably paid half as much again, but worth every penny for their leadership and guidance. The work was very similar, and almost as hard as that of a ripper on the coalface, a job I could not legally undertake at this time simply because I hadn't completed the statutory coalface training. I thoroughly enjoyed my time on Shaw's Level and learnt so much about mining, thanks to the help and advice of Walter and Bill, who were not only first-rate miners, but something of philosophers too. In the latter regard, I'll never forget a conversation one 'snap' time, which went something like this: "Edward, they tell me you've got a new girlfriend," remarked Walter quite earnestly. "Yes, Walter, that's right." "Is it serious then?" "Oh, I suppose so" – of course, all teenage romances are serious matters! Walter shone his lamp straight at me and remarked sagely "Remember, Edward, never marry a girl who can't lift her own weight."

Working on Shaw's Level brought me close to my grandfather John Edward Bedford, despite the fact that he had died even before I was born. In the 1920's he had driven a major roadway off Shaws's Level to give access to faces in the New Hards seam. To commemorate his effort, the roadway was officially named *The Bedford Bord*. It was still open as far as the Old No.15, at which point a pump had been installed to prevent water entering the Wheatley Lime workings some 20m below.

It was an eerie and quite spiritual experience for me when, alone, I entered this old working during one 'snap' time. Total silence, except that of dripping water, and a dank smell from the decaying timber lagging boards met my first tentative steps. I shone my light around. The steel roof girders were now thickly encrusted with rust, and thick ochre[22] leached out of the rocks by the ground waters now lined the sides of the water channel cut in the floor. There was even a weird species of toadstool, white, almost translucent, now sprouting from some timbers. I gazed around in the silence, my mind drifting back to a time some 30 years before, wondering what emotions my grandfather had experienced in driving this tunnel. I was suddenly returned to reality by the sound of a compressed air drill starting up again. My mates were back at work. Even if I'd returned late, I'm sure Walter and Bill would have understood. To them, as young lads in the pit, Johnny Liles[23] was 'the' big hitter then.

Park Mill was a relatively small mine, employing only some 400 men and therefore the coalface trainees did not have the luxury of a dedicated training face. Instead, we were thrown straight onto a production face to be trained by men who were earning their wages as contract workers i.e. on piecework. In these circumstances, it was hardly surprising that the quality of training was something of a lottery. Some of the workmen took their supervisory duties seriously, explaining and demonstrating the best practice. Others simply used trainees as a cheap pair of hands and it's no wonder that bad, indeed sometimes dangerous, habits were passed on. Irrespective of the standard of training, I relished being plunged into the rough and tumble of life on a production face from the outset. There's heaps of sentimental claptrap written and spoken now, mostly by people who have never even worked in a pit, let alone on the coalface, about the comradeship of miners underground. There is a grain of truth in that, but, believe me, piece workers, in the main, look after No.1 first. That's only human nature, isn't it?

Although the haulage systems at Park Mill were modern and efficient, coalface operations were still those a miner working shortly after the 1st World War would have recognised. The coalgetting system was a longwall advancing method in which a coalface 200 yards (183m) long was advanced daily by some 5ft 6 inches (1.68m). The face was reached by the main gate 12ft (3.6m) wide at the centre of the face and two tail gates 6ft (1.8m) wide at either extremity. The main gate housed a 26inch (0.66m) belt conveyor to move the coal outbye and a set of rails to facilitate the transport inbye of girders, timber and materials required in driving and maintaining the gate. Also along this gate ran the electricity cable and the water and a compressed air pipe ranges. This roadway also served as the intake airway carrying fresh air to the face. However, the two tail gates were only equipped with rails to allow timber (props, lids and bars) to be trammed[24] to the face using tubs and bogies, and a compressed air pipe range. These gates acted as the return airways from the face.

The production cycle was based on a 3 shift system. Coal was removed from the face, in an operation known as filling, and this took place on the day shift, commencing at 7.15am and finishing a 2.45pm. During the afternoon shift, from 2.00pm to 9.30pm, there were two main operations. These were ripping, whereby the gates were advanced and also belt turning, an operation to advance the face conveyor and extended the gate conveyor to keep pace with the face advance. The night shift, from 10.30pm until 6am, was principally set aside for coal cutting, although on some faces this had commenced in the afternoon shift. The face borers, who drilled shot holes in the coal, worked a split shift commencing at 11.00am. All the above operations were contract work. The only face workers, not on piecework were the under-officials. The Deputy[25] was the person statutorily in charge of the district, including the coalface, and the Shotfirers[26] whose job was to use explosives to break down the coal.

To be a regular coal filler (usually abbreviated to filler) was really the 'plum' coalface job on account of the work being carried out on the day shift. I was lucky that I had a steady, sensible supervisor when I undertook training for this work, my first coalface operation. Charles Sykes, universally known in the pit as Charlie, was old enough to be my father – indeed I used to go out with his elder daughter Joan. Fortunately, he never held that against me! Charlie's 15yard (13.7m) long stint (working place) was about in the middle of the right hand side of the South 2 face. It was with some excitement that I first crawled along the stationary face conveyor, immediately behind Charlie, throwing my shovel, hammer and pick ahead of me. Eventually we arrived at Charlie's working place. We squeezed in against the gummings[27] on the gob[28] side of the face conveyor belt since it

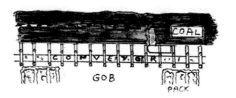

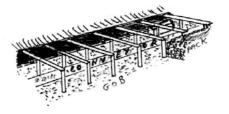

PLAN AND PERSPECTIVE OF COAL FACE

COAL CUTTING SHIFT

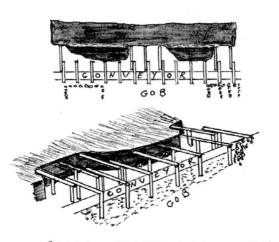

PLAN AND PERSPECTIVE OF COAL FACE

COAL FILLING SHIFT   E.G.H 2007

196

was impossible, initially, to get on the face side due to the explosives having blown down heaps of loose coal.

Eventually, the belt started and we shovelled into the smashed up coal, loading it onto the 18 inch (0.46m) wide belt, which ran directly on the floor. Having shifted sufficient coal we could then cross over the belt to the face side. From there, we dug our way to reach the solid coal some 5feet 6inches (1.7m) forward of the belt – this was known as 'breaking in'. From that point we could now work our way, with pick and shovel, along the face parallel to the belt. Every yard we cleared along the face, Charlie made me set 2 wooden props at right angles to the face, the props supporting a timber bar. In this respect Charlie was careful. Many men, in their eagerness to take advantage of the belt running (stoppages were commonplace) carried on filling leaving several yards of unsupported roof – an extremely dangerous practice. Fillers invariable hoped that the belt would run continuously so that they could work at a steady pace. Wearing only a singlet, sweat would trickle down our faces and bodies leaving white rivulets on our otherwise totally black bodies. Park Mill was by no means a hot pit and the strong ventilation current blowing along the coalface, enough to cause our singlets to flap gently, soon made us shiver during periods of enforced inactivity due to a belt stoppage.

Snap time, when the belt officially stopped for a mere 20 minutes at 11am, allowed us to wrap up in our jackets, eat in the working place and then to lay down, close our eyes, and grab a few minutes rest. All too soon, the belt would restart and the slog would be underway once more. Looking back[29] up the stint into the huge void we'd created was enough encouragement to raise our game again. After a while, I shone my light ahead and I could now see the cleared face of the adjoining stint. One final effort and we'd broken through. I know that shovelling 15 tonnes of coal for a shift, the routine only broken by setting timber and knocking the 'backs'[30] off with a pick sounds monotonous, yet, curiously, I found it satisfying. The working height of 34 inches (0.85m)[31] I found comfortable for kneeling throughout the shift, although, to relieve the occasional ache, from time to time I'd shovel lying on my side. Incidentally, I soon abandoned my regulation issue miner's helmet and purchased a cloth type from the Co-op to allow me the bit of extra headroom. This unofficial headgear, common amongst face workers, frowned upon, but tolerated by management, afforded absolutely no protection.

My face training as a filler completed, I was now a market man. That meant, I hadn't a regular stint and simply had to take what was offered each shift. That usually meant taking over, temporarily, from an absentee. In view of the arduous work, absenteeism amongst face workers was high, Mondays in particular. Some stints were relatively straightforward, others, where the conditions had become difficult due to adverse geological conditions were a sore trial. I absolutely hated working in the stints, which were passing through a fault. The roof was tender and the fault slickensides, from which huge blocks of rock could fall at anytime were absolute death traps; one had to be eternally vigilant. The pit was actually affected by quite a few geological faults, due, no doubt, to its close proximity to the axis of the Pennine Anticline.

My vocabulary, in particular those words and phrases to express anger or frustration, received many colourful additions whilst on the face. Enforced delays, through, for example, belt stoppages due to problems outbye, belt breakages and waiting for timber were the causes of much cursing and swearing and it seemed to be only the devout chapel goers who resisted the temptation. Even they succumbed in spirit by concocting oaths such as *paraffinoilcan* - Charlie's brother Harold, a Methodist Lay Preacher, was fond of this one. On the other hand, when things were going well, filling, although a shattering physical experience could be remarkably stress free. Often there were periods of eerie silence only marginally disturbed by the belt's light swishing sound. The smell of newly broken coal still releasing a whiff of explosive fumes wasn't at all offensive to the nostrils. I often lay quietly on the slightly damp floor when taking a breather, reflecting that literally millions of tons of rock were between me and the surface. Some people, I know, would suffer acute anxiety, even fear, in these claustrophobic conditions, but luckily for me this never arose.

Pits were extremely dangerous places and the threat of explosions of firedamp (methane), which in the 19th and early 20th centuries had been responsible for huge losses of life[32] had never been entirely eliminated. Park Mill was a safety lamp mine where naked lights were prohibited. It was against the law to take matches and smoking materials underground and anyone found to be in possession risked a heavy fine by the management, dismissal or the ultimate sanction, prosecution in the courts. Many men overcame the temptation to smoke by taking snuff and chewing tobacco. I had brief spells of each, but never became addicted to these practices.

Falls of ground, particularly on the face accounted for many serious accidents, however, it was not only face workers who were at risk of severe injury and death. While I was working at Park Mill two deaths occurred in relation to haulage, both to very experienced workmen. In one case, the foreman underground fitter, Walker Leather, was killed whilst inspecting the main conveyor drive in No.2 East Bord and, in another incident, Archie Cook[33] lost his life, being crushed when working on the diesel locomotive haulage. During my time at Park Mill colliery I was lucky that I never suffered a serious injury[34], but of course, I received my quota of bumps, bruises and cuts, which were simply commonplace.

Technical College studies had one great advantage. Attendance was compulsory during the autumn, winter and spring terms, therefore day release students, like myself, avoided being consigned to permanent afternoon or night shifts in this period of the year – yet a further incentive to keep up the studies. However, we became fair game during the summer months, for there always seemed to be something of a shortage of volunteers for these unsocial shifts. Immediately after the pit holidays, it came as no surprise when it was suggested that I might like to widen my face experience by training and working as a coal cutter on the night shift – the fact that there was a manpower shortage never got a mention. In truth, I was also a little surprised and relieved that my 'call up' hadn't come some weeks earlier, immediately Tech had finished. In reality, I hadn't any choice in the matter and so nights it was. I cannot think of anything worse than going to work when everyone else is switching off and going to bed. What's even worse, night shift working also messes up the weekends completely. Try as I might, I couldn't find one redeeming feature of this dreadful shift.

Park Mill pit used either Anderson Boyes (AB) 19 inch or British Jeffery Diamond 'Ace' coal cutters[35] to cut a slot 5feet 6inches (1.7m) deep and 6inches (9cm) wide in the fireclay immediately underlying the coal along the whole of the face length. The purpose was to provide a second 'free face' under the coal to improve the explosive blasting efficiency. The machines were built in 3 sections with an overall length of some 3m. The front section housed a ratchet driven drum upon which a 25m steel cable was wound and the machine's hand controls were mounted externally on this section. The middle section was a 550 volt 60 hp 3 phase induction motor. The rear section was the gearbox, which powered the cutter chain mounted on a substantial jib set perpendicular to the machine's long axis when cutting. Coal cutting was the epitome of mechanical brute force. Initially, the cable drum was put in neutral and the cable then run out from the drum and anchored along the face with a steel derrick set between roof and floor. The cutter chain was engaged, the cable tightened and gradually the machine inched itself forward, the rapidly moving picks of the cutter chain ripping out a slot in the fireclay.

There were usually 3 men in the cutting team. The 'machine man' drove the cutter and was in charge. Two men then followed the machine, one whose job it was to hammer thick wooden chocks into the slot at approximately metre intervals to prevent the coal dropping and therefore breaking the already drilled shot holes. Without doubt the third man had the worst job. Using a flat shovel with a handle almost 2m long he shovelled out the

*Coalface typical of those at Park Mill Colliery with
Anderson Boyes coal cutter*

remaining cuttings, known as 'gummings' from the back of the slot and threw them into the 'gob'[36]. Manoeuvring the long shovel in such a confined space was an art I never fully mastered and my knuckles regularly received cuts and bruises from hitting the sharp coal edge. The operation was known as feying[37] and one to be avoided if at all possible. During my coal cutting training I was given some opportunity to drive the cutter but I spent most of my time behind the machine in an atmosphere so thick with dust[38] I could barely see my hand in front of me. This was, without doubt, the low point and unhappiest time of my mining career – a terrible job, a dreadful shift – I simply couldn't wait for Tech to start again.

Another summer break from Tech saw me ripping on the afternoon shift. A comfortable lie in bed in the morning was some consolation, but having to don mucky pit clothes and be lowered down the shaft at 2 o'clock in the afternoon on a beautiful warm sunny day was hard to take. I was teamed up with

Edward Dransfield, who I already knew well, since, for several years he and his wife Jean and their two boys, Paul and Robert, had lived next door in Cuttlehurst. Edward was the left hand tailgate ripper on the South 4 face and his previous mate had recently left the pit. I got on well with Edward who, during snap times, regaled me with stories of his World War II exploits as a tank driver in North Africa, Italy and Europe. The fact that he'd come through those great dangers unscathed filled me with confidence when working alongside him.

Waiting to go underground on the afternoon shift. Myself in non-regulation headgear

The ripper's job was to advance the gate to keep up with the advancing face – essentially tunnelling. Arriving at the face, our first task was to set a double line of 'breaking off' timbers in the face to delineate the direction of the gate and to prevent any sideways overbreak i.e. we wanted to ensure the gate remained at the chosen 6feet (1.8m) width. We then used a rather primitive compressed air percussive drill to place 4 shot holes to a depth of 5feet 6ins (1.68m) into the 5feet (1.52m) thickness of rock[39] overlying the coal seam. The technique was a simple one. The drill was supported on one man's shoulder and rested on several thicknesses of hessian to afford some protection, whilst the second man stood behind the first and pushed the drill as hard as possible.

Health and safety considerations were non-existent. Imagine what it must be like to have a 'road drill' within a few inches of the ear with no ear mufflers – it's no wonder I'm now somewhat deaf in my right ear. The dust created was absolutely horrendous, for there was no attempt at dust suppression – our only protection was a small tin mask lined with a token gauze filter. No doubt the large dust particles were trapped, but the lethal micron sizes would pass straight into the lungs. The title of this chapter implies that everything in a coal pit is black. Not strictly true! The rock overlying the coal seam was grey coloured hard shale, bordering on siltstone. At the end of their respective shifts, rippers were always grey, fillers always black!

The drilling now completed, Edward and myself ate our 'snap' during which time we hoped the Deputy would be along to charge the holes and blast down the rock. When the time came to fire the shots we crawled into the face and lay down some 10 metres or so from the gate. A couple[40] of massive explosions and a huge rock pile blocked access from the gate into the face. Now the very hard graft commenced. Around $10^1/_2$ tonnes of rock had to be shovelled into the gob and packed tight against the roof. Larger pieces of rock were manhandled to build face pack walls to prevent the loose rock spilling over into the conveyor belt track. The broken rock being cleared and packed into the gob, our final task was to emerge back into the gate to bar down any loose rock. The gate, being only relatively narrow and combined with strong rock made the roof self supporting – only rarely had we to set timber supports.

My 20 shifts ripping training was soon over and I feared that I would have to go on the market again. Much to my surprise however, the afternoon Overman, Walter Skeldon, simply continued to despatch me with Edward as usual. Together, we made a decent team and I can't ever remember an exchange of cross words.

Being a contract faceworker was strenuous in the extreme and I'm sure I could not have lasted in that work for more than a few years. I saw many men whose health had been broken by the time they reached their mid 40's or early 50's. Indeed, the vast majority of that age group had been forced to leave the face and were now employed as 'datlers' underground or even reduced to 'light duties' on the surface. Even as a fit young lad my homeward journey on the bike was often a struggle, for most of my energy had been dissipated underground and I'd hardly anything left to turn the pedals and so defeat the usual nagging westerly breeze. The pain seemed to evaporate, temporarily at least, when collecting my wage on a Friday. I'll never forget the thrill of receiving my first paypacket to contain three £5 notes – the large white ones with copperplate black print. To be earning £15 a week as a lad in my late teens placed me amongst the country's high earners. The weekly earnings of a football star in those days was, I believe, capped at just £12-10s-0d (£12.50). How times have changed!

When on the day shift, it could be something of a trial to arrive home at 3.15pm, then rush a bath and grab a bite before going out to catch the 5.10pm bus to Barnsley Tech. Even on miserable, cold, dark winter's evenings I usually managed to resist the temptation to skip classes. These started at 6pm and with one break lasted $2^1/_2$ hours. Given the fact that I'd been up since 6.15am and done a shift on the face, the urge to drift off to sleep during the teacher's explanation of some point in calculus or conic sections was overwhelming. I usually managed to keep awake, but finally gave in on the bus journey home when I'd doze off for a few minutes.

When I first started work in the pit I hadn't the slightest intention of going to university, but this changed when I met Bernard Lockley, who came to work at Park Mill during his summer vacation. Bernard seemed to have a good life as a mining engineering student at Leeds University and appeared to be well placed to make a worthwhile career in the industry. He explained the ins and outs of how to approach the university of ones choice for a place and how it was necessary to have good 'A' levels, a prerequisite to winning a scholarship. In those days, passes at 'A' level did not automatically guarantee the award of a grant, but scholarships were competitive and awarded on merit following an interview. A letter direct to John T. Whetton, Professor of Mining Engineering at Leeds University resulted in me seeing him one evening. At our first meeting, initially I felt overawed, but his friendly manner soon put me at ease. I was thrilled to be offered a place and he recommended that I apply for an NCB Scholarship.

Eventually I was called for interview for the Northeast Region 'qualifiers' at the NCB Division headquarters in Doncaster. On entering the boardroom I was confronted by about 7 smartly dressed men sitting behind a massive polished table, but I was reassured to spot one friendly face – yes, Prof. Whetton. He, clearly, had taken to me since he farmed the questions very well and I spent most of the interview talking about music. The result delighted me and I was through to the national finals to be held at Birmingham University. This time, however, I didn't feel as though I'd done myself justice and my instincts were right – no award. I was disappointed and received a letter from Prof. Whetton expressing his 'condolences' and also assuring me that the offer of a place stood. Simply because I didn't know the system well enough, I had made the mistake of failing to apply for a West Riding County Major Scholarship as an insurance. The County interviews had taken place well before the NCB interviews and it was now too late to make an application since their quota of awards had already been made.

I'd learnt a hard lesson and the following year my County application was in early. I was thrilled to win a County Major scholarship and, without hesitation, I accepted immediately. Some weeks later, I derived tremendous satisfaction turning down the invitation for the NCB scholarship interview! Shortly after that, the icing on the cake! I'd also been awarded the Walter Hargreaves[41] Scholarship by the Mining Department of Leeds University.

October came and I had handed in my lamp check for the last time and the following week returned to collect my final paypacket. Light of heart, I walked away from the pay office window and my mind flashed back to that morning when I walked through the pit gates for the first time. Back then, I'd hardly heard of university, let alone met anyone, other than my grammar school teachers, who'd been to one.

Prediction is difficult, especially where the future is concerned! Never in a million years could I have imagined that some 25 years later I would be a university senior academic! Incredible isn't it? I fell into the pit to earn money with no thought of where that might lead. It was sheer good fortune that my employer was a world leader in education and training. For me, what luck!

NOTES

Chapter 1

1. Fish and chip shops were always referred to as chip holes, pronounced in dialect chip oils.
2. Jim Firth's business moved from Fleet Street to opposite the end of Dearne Terrace during the 2nd War.

Chapter 2

1. If Edward Ellis was William's father it is possible that he recognised that fact with a monetary gift.
2. The manufacture of intricately patterned cloth for waistcoats etc.
3. Norton's were one of the first manufacturers to weave using the Jacquard loom. The 1841 Census records that brothers James and Jesse Hinchliffe, my cousins 4 times removed on my mother's side, worked as a card stamper and a card lacer respectively.
4. I'm unsure of the exact relationship to my Bedford line.
5. I've been able to trace the Greens on my mothers side 12 generations back in Emley Parish to Edward Green, born circa 1600.
6. The ecclesiastical jurisdictions relating to the Townships of Cumberworth and Cumberworth Half in which Skelmanthorpe was situated were complicated and in the 19th century and earlier times split between the ancient parishes High Hoyland, Emley, Kirkburton and Silkstone.
7. In 1893 Hannah died. The 1901 census shows Edward now married to Emma, a lady some 16 years younger, who was born at Kirkburton.

Chapter 3

1. By the time of the 1891 Census he has remarried and was living in Town Street, Soothill with his wife Mary Ann, son Charles Henry aged 3 and daughter Dorothy M. 11 months old. I have been unable to find him in the 1901 Census.

Chapter 11

1. Youth organisations run by the German Nazi party.
2. The allocation of syllables to the notes of the Anglican chant.
3. Vide Chapter 10.
4. The right hand choir stall when facing the altar i.e. on the south side of the chancel.

Chapter 12

1. My report at the end of form VA I recently discovered, gave my position in English as 4th – it must have been a flash in the pan on my part!
2. In form IIIA we picked up German at which I was totally useless. Strange isn't it, as an adult I became fluent in the language.
3. An optical lantern, which could project images of pictures from a book
4. In 1993, 28 out of 34 attended a reunion and again in 2005, sadly this time with fewer in number.

Chapter 13

1. Vide Chapter 4.
2. Some years later I sat the Government's Mining Qualifications Board (MQB) examination and gained a First Class (Mine Managers) Certificate of Competency.
3. Flat pieces of wood approximately 20cm x 10cm and about 3cm thick to be wedged between props and the roof of the coal seam.
4. Wood of semi-circular cross section about 2 m long to be wedged between props and the roof of the coal seam.
5. Thick clay used to block up charged shot holes.
6. My first weekly wage as a surface trainee was £3 9s 1d (£3-45p) paid one week in arrears.
7. In my time it was Leslie Haigh who was assigned this task.
8. Inclined access tunnels from the surface.
9. Gradient of 1 in 400.
10. The area of coal allocated to the colliery.
11. Outbye – in the direction of the surface or the shaft. Opposite direction is Inbye.
12. The coal conveyor access roadways, 12feet (4m) wide, driven in the seam to the coalfaces.
13. Coalmine shaft depths were then always quoted in yards. In contrast, the Cornish tin and copper mine shafts were always quoted in fathoms (1 fathom =6 feet).
14. These clogs had wooden soles and leather tops unlike the Dutch type, which are entirely wood.
15. Always known as the box hole, pronounced box oil.
16. At this time I was earning £4-10s-0d (£4.50) a week.
17. Peter was an excellent fiddle player, also taught by Willie Kaye. Peter eventually left the pit and became a peripatetic violin teacher employed by the West Riding Education Authority.

18. A mechanical pulling device.

19. The No.1 East Bord and the No.2 East Bord were approximately parallel about 1300m apart. They were driven in a north easterly direction, which almost coincided with the full dip of the seam (1 in 9).

20. A tracked vehicle with gathering arms and a chain conveyor, which could be raised to discharge directly into the mine car.

21. I can remember 2 occasions in my career when I had to cycle to Dr Mitchell's surgery at Denby Dale for him to remove embedded flints under local anaesthetic.

22. Iron Oxide.

23. The mine management always called my grandfather John Bedford. The workmen usually called him Johnny Liles, since he had been brought up by his grandparents, Edward and Hannah Liles. Vide Chapter 4.

24. The tub or bogy is pushed manually, usually by a lad new into the pit. He's known as a timber trammer.

25. The name derives because he is deputising for the Mine Manager.

26. Explosives are used to blow things up and a Shotfirer was often referred to as a 'Blower'.

27. Fine dirt thrown back into the gob by the coalcutter's gum flinger.

28. The void left after the coal seam has been extracted.

29. The general dip of the strata was about 1 in 9 to the east.

30. Coal, which the explosives had not blown down, usually occurring roughly mid way between the 2m spaced shot holes.

31. Made up of seam thickness 28 inches (0.70m) plus 6 inches (0.15m) floor undercut by the coalcutter.

32. The worst UK disaster, in terms of lives lost, was at the Universal Colliery, Senghenydd, South Wales on 14th October 1913 when 439 men were killed in an explosion.

33. Archie had a marvellous bass voice and was a member of the renowned Huddersfield Choral Society as well as a soloist.

34. Some years later whilst an official in the 15 inch (0.38m) thick Blocking Seam at Emley Moor Colliery I was trapped in the face conveyor belt resulting in some time off 'on the sick'.

35. They were, essentially, huge chain saws hacking into the fireclay underlying the coal seam.

36. A mechanical 'gum flinger' was also mounted at the rear of the machine, which threw a decent proportion of gummings into the gob and in so doing created a continuous thick dust cloud.

37. Feying was necessary since the mine did not have a coal washing plant, simply screens for sizing.

38. The jib was fitted with water sprays but the poor design and usual low water pressure made these ineffective.

39. Known as the ripping lip.

40. The lower two holes were fired first, followed by the upper two.

41. Walter Hargreaves was a pre-nationalisation Yorkshire coalowner. A plaque inside the Mining Department records the substantial contribution that The Yorkshire Coalowners Association had made towards the new building.

BIBLIOGRAPHY

Addy, J. (ed), *A History of the Denby Dale Urban District Council*, Denby Dale Parish Council, 1995

Bromehead, C.E.N., Edwards, W., Wray D.A., & Stephens, J.V.,
The Geology of the Country around Holmfirth and Glossop, H.M.S.O., 1933

Brooke, A., *The Handloom Fancy Weavers c.1820-1914*, Workers' History Publications, 1993

Brook, R., *The Story of Huddersfield*, MacGibbon & Kee, 1968

Booth, H., *Bygone Skelmanthorpe and Huddersfield District Revisited*, Self Published, 1965

Caffyn, L., *Workers' Housing in West Yorkshire 1750-1920*, H.M.S.O., 1986

Clarke, J., *The Price of Progres – Cobbett's England 1780-1835*, Granada Publishing, 1977

Cooper, T.L., *Brass Bands of Yorkshire*, The Dalesman Publishing Co. Ltd, 1974

Deane, P., *The First Industrial Revolution*, Cambridge University Press, 1965

Giles, C. & Goodall, I.H., *Yorkshire Textile Mills – The Building of the Yorkshire Textile Industry 1770-1930*, H.M.S.O., 1992

Hastewell, C., *Nortonthorpe Mill (c. 1790 – forward)*, Self Published, Date unknown

Hey, D., *A History of Penistone and District*, Wharncliffe Books, 2002

Hey, S.E., *Photographic History of Emley*, The Enterprise Group, 1999

Hill, C.P., *British Economic and Social History 1700-1975, Fourth Edition,* Edward Arnold, 1980

Holmes, D.H., *The Mining and Quarrying Industries in the Huddersfield District*, Tolson Memorial Museum, Huddersfield, 1967

Jenkins, D.T., *The West Riding Wool Textile Industry 1770-1835,* Pasold Research Fund Ltd, 1975

Mathias, P., *The First Industrial Nation – An Economic History of Britain 1700-1914,* Methuen & Co Ltd, 1971

Heath, C., *Denby & District,* Wharncliffe Books, 2001

Heath, C., *Denby & District II,* Wharncliffe Books, 2004

Heath, C., *Denby & District III,* Wharncliffe Books, 2006

Parker, G.F., *A Description of Emley,* Self Published, Date unknown

Perkin, H., *The Origins of Modern English Society 1780-1880,* Routledge & Kegan Paul, 1969

Pobjoy, H.N., *A History of Emley,* Self Published, 1970

Reach, A.B., *A Green and Shoddy Land,* Northern Line Design, 2001 (First published 1849)

Redmond, G., *Surnames around Huddersfield,* Huddersfield Examiner, c1970

Redmond, G., *Yorkshire Surname Series Part Two – Huddersfield & District,* Self Published, 1992

Roebuck, J., *The Making of Modern English Society from 1850,* Victorian (& Modern History) Book Club, 1974

Rose, J., *The Intellectual Life of the British Working Class,* Yale Nota Bene, 2002

South & West Yorkshire Women's Institutes, *The South & West Yorkshire Village Book,* Countryside Books, 1991

Taylor, W., *South Yorkshire Pits,* Wharncliffe Books, 2001

Thompson, E.P., *The Making of the English Working Class,* Penguin Books, 1991

Wilkinson, J., *Exploring the Upper Dearne Valley,* Bridge Publications, 2002

Wray, D.A., *The Mining Industry in the Huddersfield District,* Tolson Memorial Museum, Huddersfield, 1929

A seemingly drab and unremarkable textile and mining village in the We
Riding of Yorkshire's Upper Dearne Valley is the unlikely setting for
fascinating personal story. Dr. Edward G. Hellewell, born into this workin
class environment before the Second World War, paints a picture of excitir
and challenging times growing up and working as a coal miner in, what wa
in fact, a vibrant community. A structured leisure time in orchestras, bra
bands, the church choir, cricket, swimming and cycling as well a
escapades, which energetic youngsters inevitably got up to, provide mar
amusing anecdotes. Hard work and graft were features of life in the m
20th century and the writer's experience in school and at the coalface bea
this out. The author, despite having left the district 40 years ago, ca
nevertheless claim to be a true son of the Upper Dearne Valley where all 1
great great grandparents and subsequent generations were resident. Th
book is unusual, possibly unique, since it is not simply the story of the first 2
years or so of an individual's life, but is also an account of the lives of all 2
direct ancestors back to and including his great great grandparen
generation set in the wider historical context of the times in which they live

Through study at technical college and later at university Dr. Hellewe
qualified as a Chartered Engineer and Chartered Minerals Surveyor. Lat
research in geophysics brought him the award of a doctorate. For over 2
years he was a senior university academic. Music is his major hobb
playing the violin from the age of 7 before moving to trombone in bra
bands, dance bands and orchestras, finally settling as an orchestral doub
bass player. He is also a motorcyclist and in 2003 he encompassed Cana
from the Pacific to the Atlantic in a solo ride of 9669 miles to raise money f
the Marie Curie Cancer Care charity.

£12.99

ISBN 978-0-95559-780-0

9 780955 597800

Proceeds from the sale of this book will be donated to Marie Curie Cancer Care.